PRAGUE

By Geoffrey Moorhouse
and the Editors of Time-Life Books

Photographs by Kees van den Berg

THE GREAT CITIES · TIME-LIFE BOOKS · AMSTERDAM

The Author: Geoffrey Moorhouse was born in Bolton, England, in 1931. His career in journalism began after service in the Royal Navy. For many years he was the chief features writer of *The Guardian*, an assignment that took him to 43 countries. His books include *Calcutta*—a vivid study of that city—and *The Fearful Void*, an account of his 2,000-mile journey by camel across the Sahara desert, the longest solo passage of its kind by a European. He is also the author of the volume *San Francisco* in The Great Cities series.

The Photographer: Born in 1930 in Dordrecht, Holland, Kees van den Berg was a physical engineer and meteorologist before taking up a career in photography that has caused him to travel throughout Europe, the U.S.A. and Central America. In recent years he has divided his time between employment as a sound engineer for Dutch Radio and photographic assignments.

TIME-LIFE BOOKS
EUROPEAN EDITOR: Kit van Tulleken
Design Director: Louis Klein
Photography Director: Pamela Marke
Chief of Research: Vanessa Kramer
Special Projects Editor: Windsor Chorlton
Chief Sub-Editor: Ilse Gray

THE GREAT CITIES
Series Editor: Deborah Thompson
Editorial Staff for *Prague*
Text Editor: Alan Dingle
Designer: Joyce Mason
Picture Editor: Gunn Brinson
Staff Writer: Louise Earwaker
Text Researcher: Deirdre McGarry
Senior Sub-Editor: Nicoletta Flessati
Design Assistants: Susan Altman, Paul Reeves, Adrian Saunders
Editorial Assistant: Kathryn Coutu
Proof-Reader: Aquila Kegan

Editorial Production
Chief: Ellen Brush
Traffic Co-ordinators: Linda Mallett, Helen Whitehorn
Picture Department: Sarah Dawson
Art Department: Julia West
Editorial Department: Debra Lelliot, Ajaib Singh Gill

The captions and the texts accompanying the photographs in this volume were prepared by the editors of Time-Life Books.

Valuable assistance was given in the preparation of this volume by Eva Stichova in Prague.

Published by Time-Life Books (Nederland) B.V.
Ottho Heldringstraat 5, Amsterdam 1018.

© 1980 Time-Life Books (Nederland) B.V.
All rights reserved. First printing in English.

TIME-LIFE is a trade mark of Time Incorporated U.S.A.

No part of this book may be reproduced in any form or by any electronic or mechanical means, including information storage and retrieval devices or systems, without prior written permission from the publisher, except that brief passages may be quoted for review.

ISBN 7054 0504 4

Cover: The spires of Prague's St. Vitus' Cathedral, founded in 1344, point skywards above a phalanx of red flags in a May Day parade.

First end paper: In the de luxe Hotel International on the city's northern outskirts, a partition wall of modern Bohemian glass engraved with famous landmarks of Prague's characteristic skyline, glows with light from an adjoining room. Featured from left to right are the dome of St. Nicholas' Church, a pinnacled gate-tower on the Charles Bridge and the spires of St. Vitus' Cathedral.

Last end paper: In Prague's ancient Hradčany district, patterned Renaissance plasterwork in an Italianate style embellishes an exterior wall of the Schwarzenberg Palace, built in the 16th Century for a noble Czech family and now housing the city's war museum.

THE SEAFARERS
WORLD WAR II
THE GOOD COOK
THE TIME-LIFE ENCYCLOPAEDIA OF GARDENING
HUMAN BEHAVIOUR
THE GREAT CITIES
THE ART OF SEWING
THE OLD WEST
THE WORLD'S WILD PLACES
THE EMERGENCE OF MAN
LIFE LIBRARY OF PHOTOGRAPHY
THIS FABULOUS CENTURY
TIME-LIFE LIBRARY OF ART
FOODS OF THE WORLD
GREAT AGES OF MAN
LIFE SCIENCE LIBRARY
LIFE NATURE LIBRARY
YOUNG READERS LIBRARY
LIFE WORLD LIBRARY
THE TIME-LIFE BOOK OF BOATING
TECHNIQUES OF PHOTOGRAPHY
LIFE AT WAR
LIFE GOES TO THE MOVIES
BEST OF LIFE

Contents

1	**The Pawn of Europe**	5
	Picture Essay: A Gentle Awakening	30
2	**Living from Day to Day**	41
	Picture Essay: The Playground at Slapy	62
3	**A Millennium of Changing Fortunes**	77
4	**Preserving the Magnificent Past**	103
	Picture Essay: Legacies of the Habsburgs	124
5	**A Grand Devotion to the Arts**	133
	Picture Essay: School for Champions	156
6	**Under the Communist Yoke**	167
	Picture Essay: In Celebration of May Day	186
	Acknowledgements and Bibliography	198
	Index	199

1

The Pawn of Europe

After half a lifetime of wandering the globe, I am still stirred by Prague more than by any other city I know. Part of the reason is the sheer physical loveliness that has been shaped there through the centuries. On each bank of the majestic River Vltava, as it winds northwards through the city, there are narrow, serpentine streets and ancient cobbled alleys, baroque churches with strange bulbous spires and palaces with pink tiled roofs, shady medieval cloisters and drowsy courtyards, all flowing up and along the gentle contours of the river banks. And, dominating the entire city, there is the great ridge called Hradčany (Castle Hill), crowned by Prague Castle and the lofty Gothic Cathedral of St. Vitus. It is, I think, the most dramatic skyline of any European city; I do not believe anyone can see it without remembering it for ever.

The old districts of Prague—Malá Strana (the Lesser Quarter) on the west bank and Staré Město (the Old Town) on the east—are enclaves within a busy modern metropolis that, since the early 19th Century, has spread across 200 square miles of the Vltava valley and is now the home of about 1.2 million people. Prague is not only one of the most important industrial cities in Czechoslovakia, but also, as the country's capital, the nerve-centre for most aspects of national life—from government to commerce, from higher education to the arts.

But for me, Prague also has a special poignancy, arising from the contrast between its calm beauty and the turbulence of its past. Czechoslovakia is a young country, dating only from 1918; it was created out of the ruins of the Austro-Hungarian Empire—a casualty of the First World War—and it brought together the Czechs of Bohemia and Moravia as well as their eastern neighbours and fellow-Slavs, the Slovaks, in one sovereign state. But Prague itself is an ancient city. For a thousand years it has been the capital of the Czech people, who once had a flourishing kingdom of their own, but have lived for long stretches of their history under the often oppressive rule of stronger nations.

One glance at the map of Europe will explain why both Czechs and Slovaks have spent so much of their past as someone else's subjects: they live at the heart of the continent, surrounded by powerful and acquisitive neighbours. Today, Czechoslovakia has frontiers with Poland, East Germany, West Germany, Austria, Hungary and the Soviet Union. This landlocked nation is remote from the sea: the shores of the Baltic are some 200 miles from its northern border and the Adriatic is much the same distance from its southernmost frontier. (It is therefore slightly incongruous

In the heart of downtown Prague, a lofty equestrian statue of the city's patron saint, Prince Wenceslas, looks down on the square that bears his name. The thoroughfare, an 800-yard-long avenue of shops and restaurants, is much favoured for leisurely strolls.

A cluster of pinnacles and domes rising above the rooftops of the central district vindicates Prague's reputation as "The City of a Hundred Spires". Partly obscuring the 15th-Century clock-tower of the Old Town Hall is a steeple of St. Nicholas' Church. In the background looms the gilded steel and glass dome of the National Museum, completed in 1890.

for an English-speaker to hear young Praguers addressing each other with the word *"Ahoj!"*; it means simply "hello", but is pronounced as a distinctly nautical-sounding "Ahoy!") In addition, the Czechs and Slovaks have always been relatively few in numbers, so that they could not escape the predicament of so many other small nations: having too much strategic and economic importance for others to leave them alone, yet being too weak to defend themselves.

The traditional homelands of the Czech people are Bohemia and Moravia, which make up the western two-thirds of the modern republic. The region known to the outside world as Bohemia (from the Boii, a Celtic tribe who dwelt there between about 500 and 100 B.C.) but to its inhabitants as Čechy (from the tribal name of the later Slav settlers) is a triangle of heavily wooded mountains enclosing a basin of fertile, undulating land, at the centre of which stands Prague. Immediately to the east of Bohemia lie the agricultural plains of Moravia, whose chief town is Brno.

Eastwards again, beyond Moravia, is Slovakia, a less fertile region almost entirely occupied by the rugged mountains of the Carpathian range, which reach a maximum height of 8,711 feet and peter out eventually into the plains of Hungary and the Ukraine. The languages of the Czechs and Slovaks are mutually intelligible, but the peoples remain distinct. The Slovaks have their own traditional capital, Bratislava, and, until the birth of Czechoslovakia in 1918, Prague was virtually a foreign city to them; the initiative for the creation of the new republic—and, indeed, most of the expertise and finance—came from the Czechs. Since 1969, Czechoslovakia has been a federal state and Bratislava the regional capital of the Slovak Federal Republic.

Bohemia and Moravia, the most westerly of all Slav lands, have since early times been surrounded like a peninsula on three sides by Germanic races. Slavs first arrived in what is now Czechoslovakia during the 5th and 6th Centuries A.D., migrating from their ancestral homelands between the Vistula and Dniepr rivers in search of good land for settlement. During the 9th Century, a tribe known as the Czechs built a simple wooden stronghold on the heights of Hradčany and another at Vyšehrad, two miles south on the opposite bank of the Vltava. These modest structures were the twin nuclei from which the city of Prague was to develop.

By the late 9th Century, the settlers had come together in a unified state, the so-called Great Moravian Empire, and were being converted to Christianity both by the Greek missionaries Cyril and Methodius and by a rival band of evangelists from Bavaria. But around the year 900 the Magyars—fierce Asiatic invaders who had colonized what is now Hungary—destroyed the Moravian Empire and seized Slovakia. The Slovaks were destined to be ruled by Hungarians until 1918 and for most of the intervening thousand years they were effectively cut off from their Slav neighbours to the west. Their constant subjection prevented them from developing a real élite of their own and instead confined them almost completely to the role of agricultural peasants.

By contrast, from the 10th Century onwards, Bohemia and Moravia retained their independence under the Přemyslids, a dynasty of native princes—who, nonetheless, repeatedly had to buy off the threatening German rulers whose domains all but surrounded their own. Prague had by now become the leading Czech town, largely because of its fortunate position astride the trade route from the Adriatic to the Baltic.

Most famous of the Přemyslids was Prince Václav—known as Wenceslas in English—who became a favourite saint of the Czechs and whose memory the English-speaking world still cherishes in the Christmas carol "Good King Wenceslas" (the promotion of Wenceslas to King was a modification by the 19th-Century English hymn-writer who wrote the words of the carol). Little is known of the historical Wenceslas, but he was apparently a man of great piety and learning who tried to be an enlightened ruler. His life, however, reads like a Greek tragedy: his mother murdered his grandmother and in 929 he himself was murdered by his brother Boleslav, perhaps for failing to resist the Germans effectively. And, indeed, Wenceslas' successors were more remarkable for their military prowess than for their saintliness. Although nominally vassals of the Holy Roman Emperors (who were usually Germans), the later Přemyslids made huge territorial gains in central Europe by dint of military conquest or wise marriages; at their greatest extent, in about 1300, their domains included the whole of the Czech lands and Poland, and large stretches of Hungary.

At home, however, trouble was brewing. Ever since the 11th Century, German colonists had been moving eastwards to settle in Bohemia, drawn by its under-exploited agricultural and mineral wealth; German merchants, for example, were largely responsible for developing Prague's Old Town, a district centred upon the city's ancient market-place on the east bank of the Vltava. Although the German contribution to the growth and prosperity of both city and country was considerable, the native inhabitants came in time to resent this Teutonic intrusion into their Slav nation.

In 1306 the last male Přemyslid died, to be succeeded by his brother-in-law John, a prince from Luxembourg who founded Bohemia's greatest royal dynasty, the Luxembourgs. John's son, Charles IV, presided over perhaps the proudest era in the history of the Czech nation: a time of prosperity, political stability and outstanding artistic achievement, when Prague also acquired its cathedral and university. But the friction between Teuton and Slav was heating up, and, early in the 15th Century, the Czechs staged a nationalist revolt against the domination of Bohemia's domestic affairs by outsiders. They drew their inspiration from Jan Hus, the Czech religious reformer who was executed in 1415 at the instigation of the papacy. Hus became the most revered hero of the Czechs, a symbol of resistance, whose spirit is invoked whenever the nation is threatened.

By their show of strength, the Czechs retained a kind of autonomy for a further 200 years; but in 1620 they were engulfed by the rising power of the Habsburgs, the Austrian dynasty that was soon to dominate Europe, and for the next three centuries Bohemia was ruled from Vienna.

The foundation of the Czechoslovak Republic in 1918 at last gave the Czechs and Slovaks genuine political freedom; but they were to enjoy it for a mere 20 years. Between 1939 and 1945 their country was occupied by the Nazis; and since 1948 it has been, in all but name, a dependency of the Soviet Union—a status that was harshly reaffirmed in August 1968, when Russian tanks rumbled through the streets of Prague to put an end to the Czech regime's bold, short-lived attempt to devise its own, more humane brand of Communism.

The Czechs did derive benefits from their centuries of lost independence; Prague's magnificent baroque architecture, for example, is owed directly to the munificence of the Habsburg rule. But the price they have paid has been the loss of the great intangible that free peoples have long taken for granted as part of their birthright: the liberty to follow their own national inclinations in their own country, and to be governed by whomsoever they choose. The story of Prague since 1620 is essentially the story of alien domination. Unless the outsider can grasp this fact, he or she will not understand this city, nor appreciate the wry, stoic temper of its people.

Handsome, stuccoed mansions, once the homes of Prague's prosperous Renaissance burghers, almost touch eaves across Melantrichova, a lane off the Old Town Square. Spanned by arches, the narrow byway typifies the labyrinthine street-plan of most of the city's old quarters.

The most appalling period of submission is well within living memory. On Resslova, a street in Prague's New Town, you will find a memorial to the city's darkest days: a bronze plaque affixed to the wall of the Church of St. Cyril and St. Methodius, and bearing the name of seven Czech soldiers. When Hitler's troops marched into Prague in 1939, these men had taken refuge in England; some three years later, they were secretly parachuted back into their homeland in an attempt to assassinate Reinhardt Heydrich, the brutal commander of the Nazi forces of occupation. One morning, as Heydrich was being driven into Prague from his villa on the outskirts, the parachutists threw a hand-grenade into his car and mortally wounded him.

The Nazis took a ferocious revenge. The assassins were eventually run to ground in the crypt of the church on Resslova and there they were wiped out; three were shot during the exchange of fire and four chose suicide rather than surrender. The most dreadful reprisal, however, took place at the small mining village of Lidice, only nine miles from the centre of Prague.

The Nazis picked on Lidice because they had been told that two young men from the village were serving with the R.A.F. in England. On June 9, 1942, Gestapo and SS men surrounded Lidice and dragged the inhabitants out of their houses. Every male over the age of 15—there were 173 of them—was put up against a farmyard wall and shot. The women and most of the children were sent to Ravensbrück concentration camp, where nearly all of them perished. Those children who looked suitably "Aryan"

Dressed in traditional village costumes that provide a sharp contrast to the casual urban attire of a passing shopper, sturdy Slovak farmworkers on a summer visit stroll towards the tourists' Mecca: the Old Town Hall clock.

were dispatched to the Reich to be brought up as dutiful Nazis; only 16 of them could be traced after the war. After having disposed of all the people of Lidice, the Nazis then obliterated all physical traces of its existence by blowing up the buildings and bulldozing the rubble into the ground.

But, in due course, the village was reborn. After the war, trees and a huge rose garden were planted on the original site, and a museum and a dignified memorial built; every year, visitors come to this spot from all over the world. Behind the trees a new Lidice was created: two or three rows of houses clustered around a handful of shops and a community hall.

It must be painful today for any German to contemplate the well-publicized fate of Lidice. Yet, equally, Britons cannot help but feel ashamed at the way their own nation treated Czechoslovakia. For the British government was a party to the disreputable agreement, signed at Munich in September 1938, that conceded Hitler's right to annex half of Bohemia.

In March 1938, the Nazi leader had sent his troops into Austria and within a few months he was preparing to do the same to the Czechs. A pretext was provided by unrest in the Sudetenland, a mountainous region of northern Bohemia that bordered Germany and was largely populated by Germans who, after 1918, had found themselves arbitrarily included in the new state of Czechoslovakia. The region had a strong Nazi Party, whose leader Konrad Henlein had, under the orders of Hitler, begun to demand autonomy for the Sudetenlanders. The Prague government, only too aware that Henlein's claims were merely a preamble to a military threat from Germany, decided to resist; but they might have resisted more strongly had it not been for the pressure put upon them by the French and the British, who had been playing a devious political game.

For, while claiming to support Czech sovereignty, Prime Ministers Edouard Daladier of France and Neville Chamberlain of Britain had, throughout the summer of 1938, been negotiating with Berlin, because they had come to believe that to allow Hitler to occupy the Sudetenland might finally satisfy his territorial ambitions in Europe. On September 29, 1938, the agreement with Hitler was signed in Munich. And, today, if you visit the Klement Gottwald Museum in Prague's Old Town—a dour memorial to Czechoslovakia's first Communist President—you will see upon one wall an enormous reproduction of that document. Inset into the reproduction is a photograph of Chamberlain, Daladier, Mussolini and Hitler standing around the table after the signing; as an Englishman, I am unable ever to contemplate that scene without a sense of shame.

Chamberlain flew home from Munich and insisted that he had brought "peace with honour". Over the radio he told the British people that "however much we may sympathize with a small nation confronted by a big, powerful neighbour, we cannot in all circumstances undertake to involve the whole British Empire in war simply on her account". He excused himself further with the thought that what was happening in Czechoslovakia was "a quarrel in a faraway country between people of whom we know nothing". During the following days Hitler's troops occupied the Sudetenland. Within six months the whole of Czechoslovakia was in their hands.

Long after the Second World War was over, another Englishman expressed concisely what it has meant to be a Czechoslovak during the 20th Century. In the spring of 1968, Sir Cecil Parrott, British Ambassador to Prague from 1960 to 1966, invited an academic audience in England "to imagine a Czech today who is 55 years of age. He was born an Austrian; at the age of five became a Czechoslovak; at the age of 26 became a second-class German; at the age of 32 regained his Czechoslovak status; at the age of 35 became a second-class Soviet citizen; and now suddenly at the age of 55 finds himself again at the crossroads."

I first set eyes on Prague during that same spring, when the London newspaper for which I was working sent me there to report on the Czechoslovak people "at the crossroads"—that is, under a new government that was beginning to experiment with what its leader, Alexander Dubček, called "socialism with a human face". In spite of some initial disappointment at the austerity of the Czech capital's shops and streets—and at the drabness of its inhabitants' garb—I was soon captivated by the architectural splendours of the city. The Praguers, I discovered, were bubbling with excitement about the imminent resignation of Antonín Novotný, President of Czechoslovakia since 1957 and an extremely unpopular "hard-line" Communist. Following a power struggle in January 1968 at the highest

12/ **The Pawn of Europe**

Sloping gardens lead towards the red rooftops of the Malá Strana district, which is linked to the Old Town by several bridges across the Vltava River.

levels of government between reformers and conservatives, Novotný had already been forced to relinquish his other role as First Secretary of the Czechoslovak Communist Party to Dubček, hitherto leader of the Communist Party in Slovakia.

Dubček had the reputation of being a cautious politician. Yet, he had become identified with those who advocated the liberalization of Czechoslovak society and—equally important—the radical reform of the national economy. He was an inspiring contrast to Novotný, who was the embodiment of slavish obedience to the "Party line", however disastrous in economic terms or brutal in human terms it might be. Under Novotný's predecessors, Klement Gottwald (President from 1948 to 1953) and Antonín Zápotocký (who held the office until 1957), the Czech regime had been notorious as one of the most oppressive in Eastern Europe and one of the most subservient to the wishes of Moscow. Tens of thousands of political prisoners had suffered in its labour camps; and it was in Prague that the last great show trial of the Stalinist era was held, in November 1952, when Rudolf Slánský and 10 other leading members of the Czech Communist Party were found guilty of "Titoism, revisionism and Zionism" and hanged. Prague possessed the world's largest statue of Stalin; unveiled in 1955, two years after the dictator's death, it was not taken down until 1962, long after the Soviets themselves had repudiated Stalinism. "Of course," Praguers will wryly remark, "we have always been holier than the Pope."

To some extent, that Moscow-oriented regime had been the result of yet another concession made by the West over the heads of the hapless Czechs and Slovaks. In May 1945, General Omar Bradley's U.S. Third Army swept into Nazi-occupied Bohemia from the west, but was obliged to halt at Plzeň, a mere 50 miles from Prague, so that a Soviet army, at that moment considerably further away to the east, could be the first to "liberate" the capital; this strange manoeuvre arose out of a deal made a few days previously between the U.S. and Soviet Commanders-in-Chief—with the tacit approval of their heads of state, Truman and Stalin—concerning which areas of Eastern Europe their respective armies should liberate.

When hostilities were over, Czechoslovakia's prewar President, Edvard Beneš, returned from London—where he had been in exile since 1939—and formed a government in coalition with the Communists, who had been one of the country's largest political parties before the war. Under their leader, Prime Minister Gottwald, the Communists carefully consolidated their position, infiltrating many of the democratic institutions and bringing Czechoslovakia firmly within the Soviet sphere of influence. Eventually, in February 1948, they staged a bloodless coup that placed the country completely in their hands.

By 1968, however, the Party's sovereignty was increasingly coming under threat, both from within and without. The writers of Czechoslovakia —who have traditionally believed themselves to be the conscience of their

Jewel of the Vltava

Prague has been a European political and commercial centre for more than a thousand years, thanks to its strategic position at the heart of the prosperous region of Bohemia—itself situated at the hub of the continent (inset map). The city grew up around two fortresses built in the 9th Century by Slav chieftains: one was located on the ridge of Hradčany, at the point where the busy overland trade route between the Adriatic and Baltic seas crossed the Vltava River, the other was situated at Vyšehrad, two miles upstream. By the 10th Century, a unified Czech state had emerged and the edifice on Hradčany became the seat of its rulers—a role that the castle still plays for the government of the present-day Republic of Czechoslovakia.

During medieval times, as Bohemia grew into a major European power, three large communities developed east of Hradčany: the commercial district of the Old Town; a smaller quarter across the river, known as Malá Strana (the Lesser Quarter); and the New Town, founded by King Charles IV in 1348, south of the Old Town. Charles also commissioned such magnificent landmarks as the Gothic Cathedral of St. Vitus and the fortified Charles Bridge.

In 1620 Bohemia was conquered by the Habsburg rulers of Austria and, under their aegis, splendid baroque churches and palaces were built throughout Prague. But the city did not expand appreciably beyond its medieval boundaries until the early 19th Century, when industrial growth led to the absorption of neighbouring villages. In 1922, four years after Czechoslovakia became an independent nation, the conurbation known as Greater Prague was created, with a population in the early 1980s of 1.2 million.

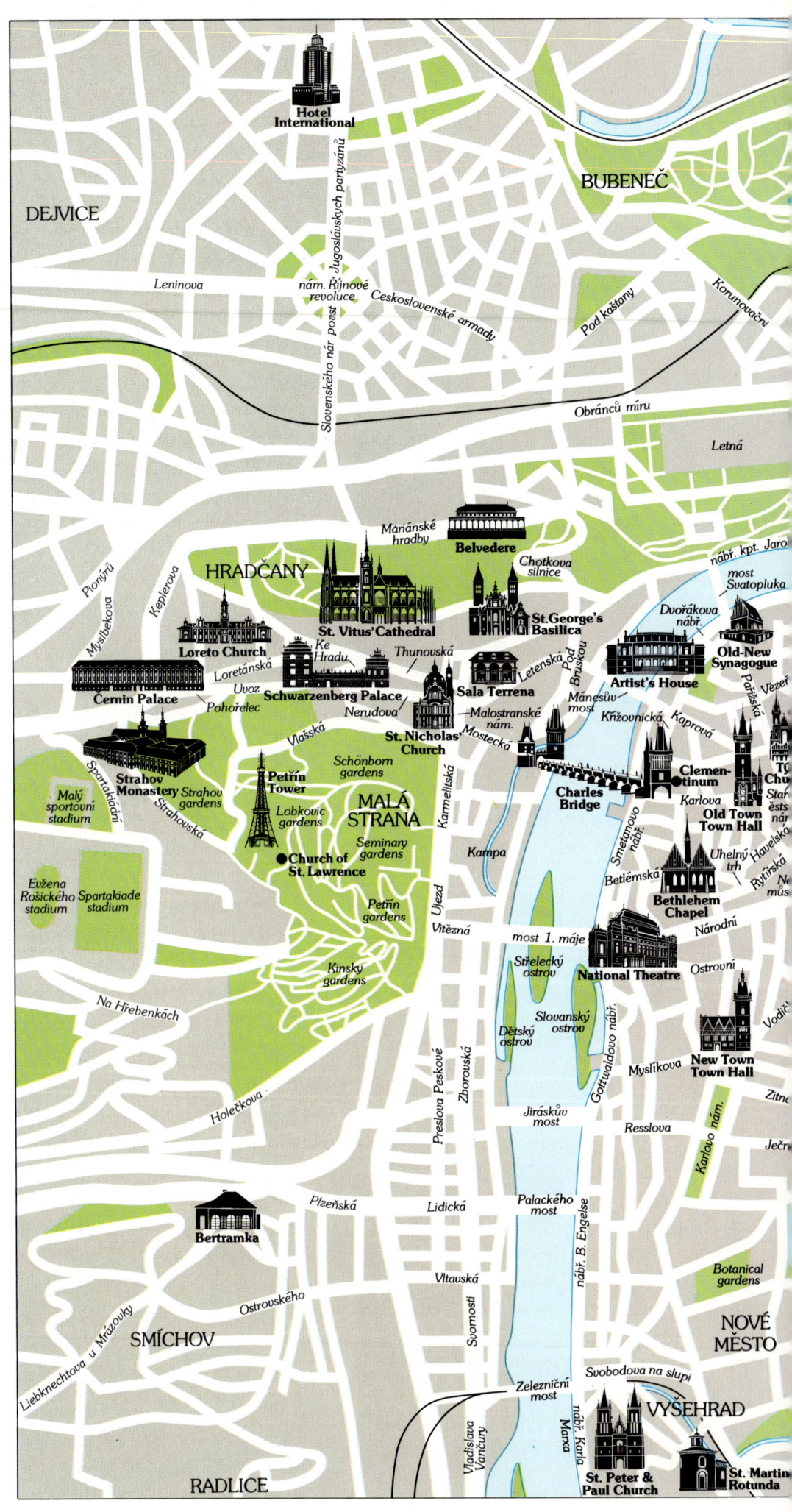

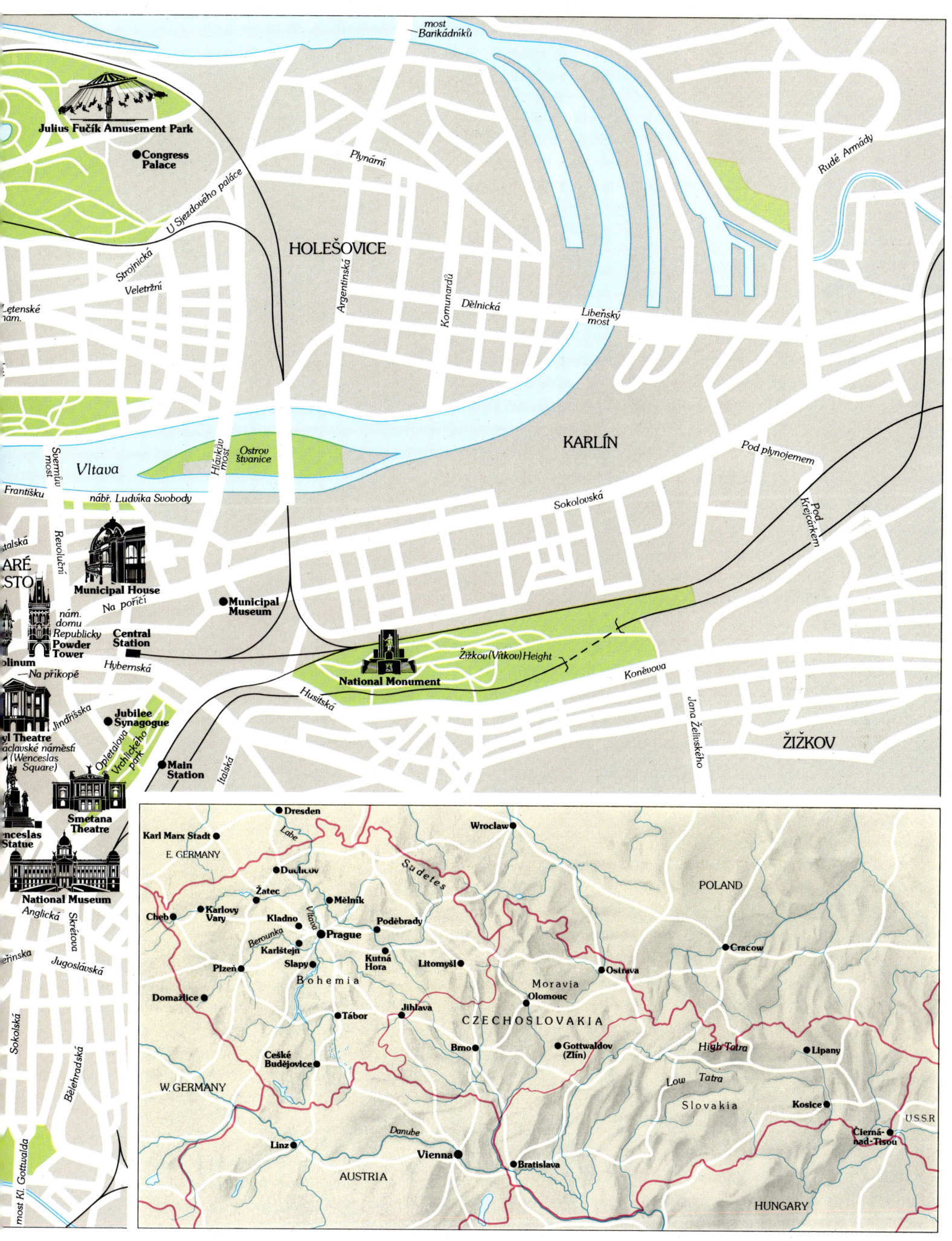

nation and have generally produced work with a high political content—were chafing against restrictions on freedom of speech; almost the only way in which they could make an "unorthodox" political comment, yet avoid the wrath of the censor, was to wrap up the message within an apparently innocuous fable. But, in 1963, the celebrated and outspoken Slovak journalist Ladislav Mňačko, in his book *Belated Reports*, took the bold step of describing openly the sufferings of his compatriots during the reign of terror in the 1950s. Astonishingly, his book got past the censor and, perhaps even more remarkably in a country of just 14 million people, it sold 300,000 copies. After that there was no holding Czech writers—the loyal Communists included. In June 1967, 400 writers gathered in Prague for their national congress, in the course of which speaker after speaker stood up to denounce the regime of Novotný—who, not surprisingly, had turned down an invitation to address the gathering. But the writers' message was clear enough to other members of the Party leadership: the time had come for a change in Czechoslovak Communism.

The students, too, had become restive, not only because of the oppressive political atmosphere but also because of the unsatisfactory conditions in which they were expected to learn. Indeed, their grievances eventually came to a head over the comparatively trivial issue of the repeated failure of the electricity supply in student hostels. On the evening of October 31, 1967, the lights failed yet again, so 1,500 students staged a torchlight procession towards Prague Castle—the residence of President Novotný. As they marched, the young people cried out Goethe's famous words: "More light! More light!"—obviously a plea for far more than an improvement in Prague's defective electricity service. A pitched battle broke out between the police and the marchers, which ended with 12 students and three policemen being taken to hospital. Once again, the incident served to remind members of the Czechoslovak government that a wind of change was blowing through their nation.

But the grievances of a few writers and students would have had little overall effect had not the vast majority of ordinary Czechs and Slovaks been suffering from the appalling mismanagement of their country's economy. From the late 1940s onwards, at the instigation of Moscow, the Gottwald regime had "purged" Czechoslovakia's industry and commerce by dismissing the "bourgeois" elements—that is, the skilled managers, technicians and small traders—and replacing them with bureaucrats of no practical experience but unquestioning loyalty to the Party. Moreover, the Kremlin decided that Czechoslovakia should become a major supplier of iron, steel and armaments for the rest of the Soviet empire; as a result, the Czech economy, hitherto both sophisticated and diversified, was ruinously distorted by the emphasis on a few heavy industries. One result was that by the mid-1960s—according to the report by a study group of the Czechoslovak Academy of Sciences—the nation's industry was, sector for sector, only between one-third and one-sixth as automated as that of the United States. This disparity was further reflected in the average industrial wage: the equivalent of about $75 per month in Czechoslovakia against $500 per month in the U.S.A. The academicians were simply pointing out what every Praguer knew only too well from his day-to-day experience: that Czechoslovakia was getting poorer, and that there was no immediate prospect of arresting the decline. During a broadcast in 1967 over Prague Radio, one of those academicians had even dared to assert openly that, were the Czech people to be asked their opinion of their government, the majority of them would register profound dissatisfaction.

When, on January 5, 1968, Alexander Dubček succeeded Novotný as chief of the Communist Party's Central Committee, he became the most powerful man in Czechoslovakia. And, all at once, the most remarkable things began to happen throughout the country.

One evening in March that year, soon after my arrival in Prague, a student took me along to a mass meeting at the Congress Palace, a grandiose 19th-Century exhibition hall standing in a park just north of the city centre. There, what seemed like tens of thousands of people had gathered to listen to an address from Josef Smrkovský, a veteran Czech Communist who had survived the Nazi occupation and the Stalinist purges to re-emerge as an ardent reformer. The crowd contained some hard-bitten working-class faces, some softer middle-class faces and, above all, row upon row of studiously hopeful young faces.

Smrkovský took the platform. He told his audience that they must work to create a socialism of the kind that the first Communists had dreamt of, a socialism that would really mean freedom and democracy for everyone. They must, he said, begin the task at once, for the present moment might be the last chance to correct the mistakes made in the Stalinist era.

A persuasive speaker, Smrkovský accompanied his words with a repertoire of gestures that ranged from the violence of the tub-thumper to the elegance of the orchestral conductor. Before long, having tossed out a proverb here and quoted some poetry there, he had those thousands of people eating out of his hand. At the end of his speech he reminded them that, throughout the previous weeks, Party committees and many other bodies at both local and national level had placed on the agenda resolutions calling for the resignation of Novotný from the Presidency as well as from the First Secretaryship of the Central Committee—"And with all my heart I agree," he added.

The crowd burst into applause that went on and on. By then, they were no doubt all accustomed to hearing their unpopular President denounced by his political opponents—but the satisfaction had obviously not worn off with the novelty. The pretty girls in the audience sparkled with merriment and kissed their boyfriends behind the ear. The middle-class faces permitted themselves small smiles of contentment. Only the working-class spectators retained impassive countenances—but they applauded all the same.

Two days later, Novotný bowed to public opinion and resigned the Presidency. In his place the Praesidium—the ruling group within the Communist Party—nominated Ludvík Svoboda, who was duly elected by the National Assembly. Svoboda had fought bravely in both world wars and served as Minister of Defence in Beneš' postwar government, but during the Stalinist purges he had been stripped of all his offices and briefly imprisoned. Although the elderly Svoboda was little more than a name to most Czechs, his re-emergence as President of the Republic at least provided Praguers with the chance to make a telling play on words. "Aha," they would tell me ambiguously, "we have Svoboda again." The name means "freedom" in Czech.

At that point, I had to return to England for a while, and so I left the Czechs with their hopes set upon a social and political system that would perhaps be unparalleled in the world. Dubček himself had pointed the way by the suggestions he had publicly made during his first few weeks of office: that the victims of past purges should be fully rehabilitated; that his country's farms should be controlled by farmers, rather than by *apparatchiks* who knew little about agriculture; and that, above all, the Czech economy should not be subservient to that of the Soviet Union. When speaking of foreign affairs, Dubček reaffirmed Czechoslovakia's allegiance to the Warsaw Pact, but spoke more gently about West Germany than was usual among national leaders in Eastern Europe.

This sane liberalism seemed to be the temper of everyone I had met during my first stay in Prague. And although they were rebelling against 20 years of Communism in its most dogmatic and oppressive form, they showed no wish to abandon its basic philosophies. I searched very hard for Czechs who were eager to adopt the Western capitalist approach to politics and society, but found none. "There is something better than either capitalism or Moscow-style Communism," I was told. "It is called socialist democracy, and we are going to try to make it work." As I left for the airport, one young man gave me a message: "Tell them in England that we are making an experiment for the whole world."

When I returned to Prague in June 1968, the city was basking in much more than its customary midsummer warmth. Dubček had been as good as his word and major reforms were taking place. Former political prisoners were now the heroes of the hour. New economic legislation allowed for limited private enterprise, something that had been almost entirely forbidden in Czechoslovakia after the Communist takeover in 1948. But most intoxicating of all for the Praguers were the new legal guarantees of freedom of speech and freedom of assembly, for whatever reason.

Journalists in particular were making the most of this new freedom to say what they liked and, as a result, the circulation figures of newspapers

Saluted by members of Czechoslovakia's pro-German minority, who are being held back by a cordon of soldiers, Hitler stands in triumph at a window of Prague Castle, residence of the Czechoslovak President, the day after German occupation of the city on March 15, 1939.

shot up to levels Prague hadn't known for years. When, in September 1967, the weekly journal of the Czechoslovak Writers' Union, *Literární noviny* (Literary News), was closed down by the censors, its average print run had been 150,000 copies. But when it re-emerged as *Literární listy* (meaning much the same) after Dubček took over, 300,000 copies were being printed. Even then a copy was practically unobtainable outside the city centre, so eagerly did Praguers rush to buy it from the news-stands in order to find out what new revelation was being made about the evils of the old regime, or what suggested reform was being put forward for the consideration of Dubček and his colleagues.

In Prague that summer, politics had quite simply become a universal obsession. In the Viola Poetry Club, a popular gathering-place for intellectuals located on the fringe of the Old Town, even verse was for the time being forgotten, as young people crammed the place night after night, sipping coffee or wine and gobbling ice cream at the little tables, their heads together over some exciting new analysis of the situation.

The first inkling that anything might go amiss with Czechoslovakia's experiment in "socialist democracy" came in the middle of July 1968, when the leaders of several of her Warsaw Pact allies—the Soviet Union, Poland, Hungary, Bulgaria and East Germany—met in Warsaw and drafted a stiff letter to the Czechoslovak Communist Party. It described the situation in Czechoslovakia as "absolutely unacceptable for socialist countries". The Czech reply was polite but conceded nothing. Later, Dubček appeared on television and announced that the Czech leadership was following the will of the Party and the people; its legislative programme was based on the liberal principles set forth during the previous six months, and from these it would not deviate an inch.

The following day, messages of support for Dubček began to roll into the Communist Party headquarters and the Prague newspapers from all over the country. In my hotel, about 30 of the staff stopped work and held an impromptu meeting to decide upon an appropriate gesture. The desk clerk took the chair and asked the chef in his white hat, the boilerman, a bevy of chambermaids and waiters, and all the others what was their will. It was decided to send the Party leaders a telegram stating that, in one establishment at least, people were keeping their fingers crossed for the success of the reforms. "All over the country," a receptionist told me, "people are holding meetings like this now"; and, with a beam of solidarity on her face, she tripped off to attend to the hotel guests.

That week, the Czechs had good cause to be nervous about the future of their new regime. The annual Warsaw Pact manoeuvres had just been held in Czechoslovakia, during which the armies of half a dozen of the nation's military allies had thrashed around the countryside in mock combat. By early July most of them had gone home, their exercises finished

An exuberant crowd greets Soviet soldiers as they drive through the streets of Prague on May 9, 1945, bringing liberation to the city after six years of German occupation.

—all but the soldiers of the Red Army, who seemed to be taking an unnecessarily long time to pack up and go. Every day, the Prague newspapers carried articles making it abundantly clear that the Czechs felt they had played host to their allies for quite long enough. And in the same papers appeared cynical little cartoons that tried to laugh off a growing fear that the Soviets intended to use their military presence to intimidate Dubček and his fellow reformers.

Suddenly, the Czech Praesidium was summoned to meet its Soviet opposite number, the Politburo, at the little town of Čierná-nad-Tisou on the Czechoslovak–Soviet border. Dubček refused to negotiate while Soviet troops remained in his country and so, at last, the unwelcome guests slowly began to leave. Yet, despite this apparently hopeful sign, the atmosphere in Prague remained electric. For the Czechs now realized beyond any doubt that the proposed meeting at Čierná-nad-Tisou marked a crisis point. They feared that their leaders were about to be bullied, man to man, into changing their ways. At this moment, when their national destiny was once again balanced on a knife-edge, the Czechs must have felt as helpless as their forefathers had so often done. But the impulse to do something to support their leaders could not be suppressed.

Once again, the writers took the initiative. On Friday, July 26, three days before the talks at Čierná-nad-Tisou were due to begin, a special four-page edition of *Literární listy* appeared. The front page was occupied by a lyrical poem expressing hope for beloved Czechoslovakia, written by the veteran Czech poet, Jaroslav Seifert, and by a manifesto in support of Czechoslo-

Unveiled in 1955, the city's memorial to Josef Stalin—showing the Soviet leader backed by workers, peasants and soldiers—was the largest monument to the dictator ever built. Nicknamed the "Bread Queue" by irreverent Praguers, the lofty statue dominated the northern embankment of the River Vltava until 1962, when the Czech government ordered it to be blown up (inset) as a gesture towards the "de-Stalinization" of the Communist bloc.

vak self-determination by the playwright Pavel Kohout. The remaining three pages of *Literární listy* that day were filled with the names of people who subscribed to the sentiments of the poem and the manifesto. Some were well-known; others were obscure, ordinary citizens. All of them knew, when they allowed their names to be published, that if things were to go badly for Czechoslovakia during this latest crisis in its history they would be marked men and women.

The same is true of all the other Praguers whose names eventually became associated with that historic edition. For, wherever *Literární listy* was sold that afternoon in Prague, tables were set up with piles of foolscap paper upon them and each purchaser of the newspaper was invited to sign his or her name. When the weekend was over, all the signatures were to be collected and taken to the Praesidium, so that Dubček and his colleagues would know that the people of Prague were behind them when they went to talk to the Soviet leaders. It is said that, in the end, 100,000 signatures were mustered from a city whose population numbered only 1.2 million. I can only report that at every news-stand that I passed in downtown Prague that day there were lines of people up to a hundred yards long, shuffling quietly forward to add their names to the sheets. I don't expect I shall ever see anything like it again.

The text of Pavel Kohout's front-page manifesto is almost unknown outside Czechoslovakia, but it deserves a much wider audience. The voice of a small and civilized nation speaking from its heart in time of trouble, it contains much that others should remember. Here is part of what it said:

"Dear Comrades—There have been many times in the history of the human race when a few men have decided the fate of millions. This is another of them. It is difficult for you, and we want to make it easier for you by our support. The history of our country in the past few centuries is the history of restriction. Several times we have stood on the brink of catastrophe . . . Now the moment has come when we can prove to the world that socialism is not only a temporary solution for underdeveloped countries, but the only way for the whole of civilization.

"It is your task to show the Russian Communist leaders that the democratization of socialism in our country must to the very end correspond to the interests of our country and to the interests of all progressive movements in all continents.

"It would be a tragedy if any personal feelings of yours prevailed above the responsibility you have to this nation. Do not forget you are part of it. Act, explain, and together stick to the way we have already trodden and from which they shall not take us alive. We shall in the next few days, hour after hour, follow your negotiations. We shall be awaiting news of you. We are thinking of you. You must think of us. You are writing a page of Czechoslovak history. Write it with care but above all with courage. It will be our tragedy if we lose our last chance. We believe in you."

A young woman at *Literární listy*'s office translated the manifesto for me so that I could cable its contents to my newspaper in London. We sat amid a hubbub of editorial staff and printers who were dashing around putting the finishing touches to the historic edition before it went to press. When, after a couple of hours' hard labour, the translation was finished, I offered the woman payment at what was then the going rate for such work in Prague. It was a sum that would have bought her a couple of summer dresses in one of the city's smarter stores, but she refused it with much dignity. "No, thank you," she said. "This is for democracy."

At Čierná-nad-Tisou, where the Czechoslovak Praesidium and the Soviet Politburo met for four days in the hastily redecorated railwaymen's club, a great deal of browbeating went on, although the details have never been properly told. After the Czech leaders had returned to Prague, President Svoboda appeared on television and asserted: "We shall not depart from the path on which we have set out." But he spoke with the manner of a man who picks his words carefully. His face had scarcely faded from the screen before a long column of angry and suspicious students began marching down Wenceslas Square, chanting "We want freedom" and

In a show of force intended to intimidate would-be opponents, Soviet tanks line a central Prague street.

Soviet Occupation

In the early hours of August 21, 1968, Warsaw Pact forces invaded Czechoslovakia to restore the Soviet hegemony that was threatened by the policies of the reformist leader, Alexander Dubček. Within a matter of hours, armoured vehicles lined the streets of Prague, and Dubček and his colleagues were arrested. Shocked and angry, the capital's citizens expressed their hostility to the invaders with anti-Soviet posters and graffiti, mass demonstrations and acts of sabotage; in the ensuing disorders 20 Praguers were killed. But the resistance was doomed: within six days the Czech government was pressured into submission to the Moscow line and the city relapsed into a state of dejected calm.

A Red Army officer bluntly ignores a woman's impassioned reproaches as a Czech crowd confronts the crew of a Soviet tank in the heart of the occupied city.

A young Czech tries to immobilize a Soviet tank by hooking the vehicle's towing cable into its tracks in Wenceslas Square, the scene of bitter fighting.

handing out leaflets that invited citizens to a meeting that was to be held in the Old Town Square later that evening.

Throughout the centuries, in good times and bad, Praguers have congregated on the cobble-stones of the Old Town Square to demonstrate their feelings—and on the night of August 1, 1968, they packed the square in their thousands. Dozens of young people perched themselves upon the great statue of Jan Hus—the man who, 550 years before, had inspired his compatriots to rebel against foreign domination. The crowd called for the Praesidium to come out and explain itself; and presently Josef Smrkovský appeared on a balcony high above them. Obviously a tired man, he tried to explain that things were not so bad as they had been represented, and he begged his audience to be calm, to forget their differences with the Russians and to think of co-operation instead. There was some applause, but there were sounds of scepticism and derision too. Most of the crowd, however, stood silently in the night and, when the meeting broke up, dispersed with an unnatural lack of animation.

But two days later the Praguers' spirits rose again. The leaders of the Warsaw Pact countries met at Bratislava, on Czechoslovak soil, and there pledged to respect, subject to a few modest conditions, Czechoslovakia's "equality, sovereignty, national independence and territorial integrity". When the Bratislava communiqué was announced, a great wave of relief spread over the Czech capital. Practically everyone realized, of course, that from then on their government would have to proceed more cautiously in its "experiment for the whole world"; but at least, it seemed, they were now assured of being allowed to proceed. The very last Soviet soldier had left Czechoslovakia on the day of the Bratislava agreement. Praguers at last felt free to begin their summer holidays, and they headed for the countryside in droves. We foreign journalists also decided that the crisis was over and took the earliest possible plane home.

I was on holiday in a remote part of the English countryside when I heard how, on the night of August 20, Czechoslovakia had been betrayed. Throughout the hours of darkness, wave after wave of Soviet troop-carrying aircraft had landed at Prague's brand-new Ruzyně Airport. Simultaneously, thousands of tanks, and trucks containing hundreds of thousands of Soviet, East German, Polish, Hungarian and Bulgarian troops, had poured over the Czech frontier at about 20 crossing points. By morning, Czechoslovakia was an occupied country.

By then, also, the leaders of its government had been seized. At Prague Castle, Soviet officials tried to persuade the aged President Svoboda to appoint a government of their choosing; he refused, and so was taken to Moscow. Courageously, he still declined to co-operate unless his colleagues were present; so Dubček, Smrkovský and others were brought to Moscow. The Czech leaders were kept in the Soviet Union for five days, until the immediate repercussions of the invasion had died down. The

Surrounded by a bed of red tulips, the first Soviet tank to enter Prague on May 9, 1945, stands outside a Czechoslovak Army barracks in the south-west of the city as a permanent monument to liberation. Guarding it during the annual Liberation Day celebrations are members of the Pioneers, the official youth organization for children aged six to 15.

world can never know the pressure put upon them, but they returned to Prague broken men. They accepted the awful logic of their position, that from then on they must perform to the letter what Moscow ordered.

Czechoslovakia had fallen victim to a perfidious, if brilliantly planned, stratagem. Its armed forces, greatly outnumbered, were ordered by the Praesidium to stay in their barracks, and the population at large could make only token gestures of defiance. The bloody fighting that had taken place in Budapest in 1956 was not repeated in Prague in 1968. Bullets did fly around Wenceslas Square and other parts of the city during the first couple of days of occupation; and a number of people were shot dead—including an 11-year-old boy who was attempting to put a Czech flag down the gun barrel of a Soviet tank. Outside the Prague Radio headquarters, some Soviet vehicles were set on fire by youths hurling Molotov cocktails. But mostly the Praguers stood bitterly in the streets, when it seemed safe to do so, and harangued the crews of the Soviet tanks that were parked at almost every corner. These young Soviet soldiers, mostly village lads of 18 or 19, were utterly bewildered by their reception. They had been told beforehand that they were going to liberate their Czech comrades from imperialist subversion and, perhaps, a West German invasion; but all they found were angry Praguers telling them to go home.

Many of the Praguers who had gone off on holiday abroad after the Bratislava agreement never came back; if they had put their names to the manifesto in *Literární listy*, they were doubtless wise to stay away. Others got out of the country during the period before the "hard-liners" took over completely and have not returned. But those supporters of reform who courageously chose to stay at home and see things out frequently became, in the months immediately following the Warsaw Pact invasion, victims of a sinister official process known as "normalization". Some were sent to prison, others lost their jobs or were evicted from their state-owned homes into less comfortable quarters; and, in order to cow the population at large, Red Army soldiers would occasionally kidnap an innocent Czech citizen, beat him up a little and dump him far from home.

For the sake of appearances—the invasion had provoked universal condemnation not only from the non-Communist world but also from Romania, Yugoslavia, and the French and Italian Communist parties—Dubček and his colleagues were allowed to stay in office for eight months but were eventually weeded out and replaced by more biddable Party members. Dubček served as Czech Ambassador to Turkey for a few months early in 1970, but eventually ended up as manager of the transport pool at the forestry department of a provincial town in Slovakia. His ignominy was complete. The Czechs were not even to be allowed a martyr to their idealistic attempts to change the world.

But, all the same, a martyr did appear: Jan Palach, a 20-year-old student of history and political science at Prague's Charles University. On the afternoon of January 16, 1969, he went to Wenceslas Square and sat down under the great equestrian statue of Czechoslovakia's patron saint. There, he poured petrol over himself and ignited it with a cigarette lighter; in spite of the fact that he suffered third-degree burns over 85 per cent of his body, Palach took three days to die. He left a note saying that, every three days, another young Czech would immolate himself unless censorship—reimposed after the invasion—were lifted. And, during the following weeks, at least 20 people burnt themselves to death in Czechoslovakia and elsewhere in central Europe.

The death of Jan Palach sparked off Prague's last collective outburst of the spirit of 1968; and, astonishingly, the authorities sanctioned the city's expression of grief. Palach was given a funeral that was attended by an estimated half a million people. The church bells of Our Lady of Týn—whose Gothic spires soar up from the Old Town Square—tolled solemnly as the interminable procession of mourners wound its way through the streets. The time at the crossroads had passed. After that, the people of Prague resigned themselves to a way of life that has been familiar to the Czechs since the Habsburgs crossed their horizon.

Today, one finds that the city has by no means been stripped of all gaiety, nor are its citizens perpetually shrouded in gloom. There are taverns, restaurants and clubs in Prague where you will find as much boisterous jollity as in any other European capital. There are the consoling visual delights of the city's old quarters. There are the political jokes; for, like the Jews, the blacks and many others, the Czechs have discovered that a sense of humour relieves the strain of being an oppressed people. One joke, so typical of their dry taste as to be classic, goes like this:

A Praguer is walking along one side of Wenceslas Square, and a soldier of the Red Army is walking along the other. Suddenly, both see a lump of gold lying in the middle of the square and rush towards it. The two arrive at exactly the same moment. "Now, comrade," says the soldier, "let's share it out like brother socialists." "No," says the Czech, "let's just go halves!"

A Gentle Awakening

Under a summer dawn, two tramcars await the first passengers of the day. Introduced in 1891, electric trams are still a mainstay of Prague's transport system.

For most Praguers, the day begins early. Factory gates open at 6 a.m. and offices start business by about 8.30, so buses, trams and trains are soon on the move, ferrying workers to their jobs. Because of the country's severe labour shortage, almost everyone belongs to the work-force—which means that many housewives must rise an hour or so early to do their shopping on the way to work, or risk finding that erratic supplies of essentials have run out by the time they leave for home. Curiously, for all the thousands of people on the move, there is little sense of frenzied rush as this city awakens to a new day. Especially in central Prague's old cobbled squares and narrow streets, where a consciousness of the past persists, the quiet grey light of early morning finds the city stirring at a relaxed pace that is entirely in keeping with its dignity.

A lamplighter douses one of the gaslamps whose soft glow still illumines a few streets in old Prague. The ornate lamp-post bears a brash modern litter bin.

In a quiet side-street a policeman turns on traffic lights that have been switched off overnight to save power.

Outside one of Prague's countless beer parlours, a driver makes his morning delivery of the world-famous beer from the town of Plzeň in western Bohemia.

A workman shovels coal—Prague's main domestic fuel—into a hotel cellar.

A woman on her way to work collects a loaf of bread—freshly delivered from one of the city's all-night bakeries—at a grocery shop that has just opened.

Shoppers attracted by a consignment of tomatoes call in at a city-centre store. Many fruits and vegetables are imported from other East European countries.

An old man who supplements his pension with a job delivering newspapers for the Post Office does his morning round in a square near Prague Castle.

As the first rays of the sun shed a golden light into Prague's busy Central Station, a railway employee discusses departure times with a pair of travellers going out of the capital before the main flow of commuters gets underway.

2
Living from Day to Day

Ever since August 1968 the citizens of Prague have had to come to terms with their dashed hopes. It is a habit that comes more readily to them than to most populations; throughout many centuries of their history, political reversals have forced the Czech people to live under the yoke of foreign domination. It seems to me that now, once again, most Praguers have shrugged their shoulders and resigned themselves to tolerating the present situation as best they can.

Perhaps not everyone felt betrayed and disappointed by the failure of Party leader Dubček's experiment in "socialism with a human face". There may even have been Praguers who sighed with relief at the return of the old doctrinaire system, finding it much more predictable and more convenient. A city official, for example, proudly told me that in a single year during the 1970s Praguers had put in 32 million hours of unpaid work; they had been organized to plant trees, to build kindergartens and, in one instance, to erect a complete shopping centre. No doubt some of these people were sincere supporters of the regime and gave up their spare time for the greater good of the community; but the vast majority of Praguers, far from exerting themselves enthusiastically in such enterprises, seem to be contributing no more effort than is absolutely necessary to get by without drawing attention to themselves.

They live from day to day, taking their pleasure where they can—in the beer cellar, at the soccer stadium or out among the beauties of the Czech countryside—and, above all, trying to keep out of trouble. In every sense of the term, they are "taking it easy". Armed with this attitude, it is possible for them to lead a pleasant enough life.

By materialistic standards, the quality of life in Prague appears to have improved considerably since 1968. There are, for example, many more automobiles on the city's streets; official sources claim a tenfold increase in the number of private cars, to more than 250,000 at the end of the 1970s. Traffic jams regularly occur along the major approach roads and on Fridays (when many Praguers head for the countryside) and Sunday evenings (when they return) police helicopters hover overhead, helping to re-route the traffic.

At the end of the 1970s, the commonest family cars seemed to be the Czech-manufactured Škodas and the Fiats built under licence in Poland and the Soviet Union. A Škoda cost the equivalent of two years' pay for the average wage-earner and the petrol to run it was at least a third more expensive than in Britain, for example. But since in most Czech families

The landlord of U Kalicha—"At the Chalice"— a popular Prague beer parlour in the New Town, draws the last half-litre (16 fl oz) mug for a table of five. Beer is the favourite drink of the Czechs and Slovaks; in terms of per capita consumption, they regularly rank among the half-dozen thirstiest nations on earth. And some of their domestic brews—the pale, strong Pilsner and Budweiser varieties, for example— are thought to be among the finest in the world.

both husband and wife work, and since rents are low and social services largely free, the cherished status symbol of an automobile is, by dint of careful saving, increasingly attainable.

The population is also much more smartly dressed. For some years now, Praguers have been almost indistinguishable in appearance from the inhabitants of Western cities—except for the fact that in Prague there is no counterpart to the small handful of Westerners who can afford to spend a fortune on exclusive designs.

Every afternoon the Slavia—a fashionable café on the east bank of the Vltava, opposite the National Theatre—is crowded with elderly ladies in fairly elegant costumes and hats who sip tea and nibble cream cakes or jam tarts, just as old ladies in Cheltenham or Vienna do at the same hour of the day. The fashionable young dress exactly as their counterparts do on London's Fulham Road, Manhattan's East Side or Rome's Spanish Steps.

The shops of Prague seem to be better stocked with luxury consumer goods than I had remembered. Young mothers proudly push their Staeger prams, fashionable imports from West Germany with transparent panels in their sides so that reclining babies can watch the world pass by—a device said to make for brighter, better behaved children. The shops themselves are changing too; gradually, the traditional small retail establishments, with assistants standing behind counters, are giving way to supermarkets and modern department stores.

But as you watch Praguers shopping for basic necessities you realize that your first impression of a much-improved standard of living does not apply to all sides of life. Largely because of widespread bad management in Czechoslovakia's publicly owned retail trade, shortages of all kinds of commodities still occur with depressing regularity. One morning, queues will suddenly form outside a handful of greengrocers' shops; the following afternoon, perhaps, a patient line of shoppers will be standing outside the general food stores. They have somehow learnt that small consignments of, say, new potatoes or canned fruit have just arrived in Prague.

Often the quality of the goods, when they are available, leaves a lot to be desired. Some of the carrots, parsnips, apples and other produce I saw at the street market on Havelská, in the Old Town, looked so withered and unappetizing that I cannot believe they would be offered for sale anywhere in Western Europe. Some of the canned foods imported from other East European countries have a reputation for poor quality and so remain on the shelves indefinitely.

Within the Eastern bloc, the standards for, and availability of, different goods can vary considerably from country to country. Travel within the bloc is comparatively easy and unrestricted, so many Praguers seem quite prepared to drive northwards for an hour and a half into East Germany in order to obtain clothing, French cheese or even such staple foods as lentils. Hungary, too, has become a popular place for shopping; you simply fly

In a butcher's shop-cum-snack-bar in the Old Town district, a white-coated assistant carries a heaped tray of smoked Prague ham, a delicacy for which the city is famed. Customers can also choose from a wide variety of sausages; steamed and served with bread and sauerkraut, they provide Praguers with a favourite meal.

44/ Living from Day to Day

to Bratislava (domestic flights are inexpensive) and then take a train for the 125 miles to Budapest. No visa is needed. So many Praguers regularly make this journey that Czech banks often run out of Hungarian currency.

These forays across the frontier also serve to reinforce the national pride of the Czechs. One day I overheard someone in a restaurant discussing a recent holiday in the Soviet Union. With mixed disgust and satisfaction she was describing how the shops in Moscow were much more poorly stocked than those in Prague. A few days later I wandered into a Prague draper's shop whose shelves and counters were loaded with bolts of cloth for every conceivable purpose. A housewife—accompanied by a friend who appeared to be French—had paused by a huge roll of synthetic fabric and was fingering it thoughtfully. "We make rugs from this stuff," she told her friend, "but the Poles come over and buy it to make into coats!"

One thing that the average Praguer shares these days with the average Westerner is his determination to make money. But in Czechoslovakia, where everyone is a state employee and private enterprise is officially forbidden, it is difficult to gain financial profit legally. The average wage for a skilled person is about 16 crowns (about $1·50) an hour, and the standard working week consists of five eight-and-a-half-hour days. Admittedly, such things as public transport and rents are infinitely cheaper than anywhere in the West, but many foodstuffs and most consumer products are significantly dearer. Consequently, many Praguers go in for "moonlighting"—illegally undertaking private work in addition to their official labours—because a single pay cheque would not enable them to live at the standard to which most people outside the countries of the Third World have nowadays become accustomed.

This form of private enterprise, both during and after working hours, is possible because the country is confronted by a chronic labour shortage, which makes it necessary for a large proportion of the city's women and elderly people to work. In Czechoslovakia, more than 80 per cent of women of child-bearing age are in full-time employment, and about 9 per cent of the labour force are persons who have exceeded the official retirement age. When making excuses for slow progress on this or that project, the authorities constantly blame the lack of manpower. At the same time, of course, "moonlighting" contributes to the low productivity of many enterprises and, as well, exacts a penalty on people's free time.

The shops of Prague are often only half-manned on Friday afternoons, because the shop assistants take turns in going out to do their weekend shopping. And at 9 o'clock on any morning of the working week, beer parlours are full of truant working people; the flow of customers does not cease until late afternoon.

Bribery—minor and major—has become rampant, as another way of boosting incomes. Plumbers, electricians and other artisans—employed,

Early morning shoppers line up patiently outside a fruit and vegetable stall on Havelská Street. Basic foodstuffs are often in short supply. When word gets out that a shop has a consignment of fresh produce, queues are quick to form.

like everyone else, either by the municipality or directly by the State—should be equally available to anyone who needs them, yet it has become difficult for a Praguer to have any kind of maintenance or repair work done unless he is willing to pay substantially more than the official rate for the job. At one time, only waiters, taxi-drivers and hairdressers assumed that they would be given a tip; but now most sections of the community expect to receive a private bonus—and in advance, as an incentive before they will perform their functions. It is common practice, also, to provide a consideration for officials if you want to get on a housing list; for appraisers of a deceased's estate, especially if you want an item to be undervalued; and even for examination tutors if you hope for a successful outcome to your child's studies. Indeed, it comes as a surprise if any individual refuses an offered tip. Doctors and dentists are likely to keep you waiting for the free treatment dispensed by the State, unless you first hand over a bottle of spirits or a carton of cigarettes.

The same climate of behaviour supports a flourishing black market in a wide range of products. The Praguer who has just bought a new car, for example, is wary of a particularly pernicious aspect of this illicit free enterprise. He will not, if he is wise, leave the car to be serviced until it has run for many thousands of miles, since the garage mechanic is quite likely to remove almost brand-new parts, for highly profitable resale, and replace them with old ones.

But the black-market trading that the foreigner is most likely to encounter concerns foreign currency. A visitor can easily obtain two to three times the official rate of exchange for his money if he pays attention to the strangers who approach him half a dozen times in the course of a day—starting with the taxi-driver who takes him from Prague's airport to his hotel. In theory, trafficking in money is illegal; in practice, it is tolerated—and, in a sense, openly encouraged—by the authorities. With the express purpose of snaring as much hard foreign currency as possible, the State has created a large chain of duty-free stores known as Tuzex; and the special Tuzex coupons—the sole currency recognized in these stores—can be obtained only in exchange for foreign banknotes. Any Czech who takes foreign currency into a bank within 10 days of acquiring it and changes it for Tuzex coupons is covered by an amnesty; and no questions are asked. If, however, for any reason his home is searched and he is discovered to have foreign currency hoarded there, he will be prosecuted for the offence.

The range of stock advertised in the Tuzex catalogue is remarkable—even if the blight of maladministration means that some of the items advertised may not actually be available at the particular store you visit. There are excellent local consumer products such as glassware, leather goods and ceramics; every alcoholic beverage I've ever heard of; chewing-gum from Denmark; tape-recorders from Japan; French cosmetics,

Spanish wallpapers, Swiss watches, tweeds from Scotland and sausages from West Germany. You can buy from Tuzex a new Renault car, an Italian washing-machine or a Scandinavian chainsaw. In fact, you can almost equip your house from top to bottom there.

Many Tuzex goods are either unobtainable elsewhere in Prague, or are infinitely more expensive; gin and whisky, for example, are about three and a half times dearer at ordinary shops. Not surprisingly, such purchases are powerful status symbols, even more so than the possession of a car. In Prague there is a special Tuzex shop that stocks nothing but blue jeans and at whatever time of day you pass it there will be a queue of people waiting to go in and buy.

The Tuzex chain was initially intended for people who possessed foreign currency that had been sent home to them by relatives living abroad—the estimated 150,000 or more Czechs who left after 1968, for example. In addition, many Czechs work abroad on a temporary basis; a technician helping to build a sugar refinery in Syria or a plant in India will have part of his wages paid to his wife and children at home, but the major part will be paid to him in Tuzex coupons, with which in due course he will return as a relatively rich man. Because so many families have two wage-earners, there is more money about than there used to be, and those who have no legitimate way to convert their cash have to rely instead on encounters with visitors from abroad. Tuzex is therefore available, in practice, to a widening cross-section of Prague's population. As a result, for those who cannot earn enough to afford the expensive goods—and for those who simply haven't the nerve to accost just anyone who looks like a foreigner—Prague's Tuzex shops represent a grotesque form of privilege, and as such are fiercely resented.

On the one hand, the authorities seem to be embarrassed by this tacit acknowledgement of the inadequacies of the Czech economy, and the stores are discreetly signposted; to make them too obvious would also only increase resentment. On the other hand, they are opening yet more shops on the ground floors of the impressive new buildings that are being erected by foreign trade corporations.

Like all the harsher facts of life in Prague, the inequities of Tuzex are hidden from the casual visitor intent on simply enjoying the splendours of the city. It is not difficult to believe that the majority of Praguers are content with their lot. The tempo of life, for example, is more civilized than in most cities of similar size. Wenceslas Square in the rush hour is as crowded as Oxford Street, or 42nd Street between Lexington and Fifth; but the people heading for the Metro stations and the tram-stops—men and women with their shopping bags and briefcases, the young people with their hands jammed into the pockets of their jeans—move at an easy pace. And surely, the visitor tells himself, only an easy-going city can devote so

Immersed in conversation, two customers await lunch in the dining room of the Europa Hotel, whose flamboyant art nouveau décor recalls a bygone era.

Relief from Care

Prague's innumerable restaurants, cafés, wine bars and taverns offer citizens welcome relief from the strains of life under a stringent political regime. The city's once de luxe catering establishments have lost much of their former flair since the advent of state ownership, but Praguers with more modest tastes can still find eating-places that provide an inexpensive filling meal of pork and dumplings, as well as quiet cafés where they can linger long over coffee and pastries. Even more popular are the taverns, where the convivial atmosphere and the strong Czech beer, often brewed on the premises, have, since medieval times, helped the inhabitants of the city to shrug off their cares.

48/ **Living from Day to Day**

A waitress at a snack-bar in the Old Town Square pauses briefly from serving lunches to chat with a customer.

In a corner of an old-fashioned coffee-house, elderly Praguers spend a tranquil afternoon reading the newspapers or gazing out across the Vltava River.

After work, friends gather for drinks at U Pinkasů—"At Pinkas'"—a 15th-Century tavern renowned for the excellence of its beer, brewed at Plzeň.

50/ Living from Day to Day

Dwarfed by giant chandeliers, Praguers dine at the spacious Municipal House, a complex of restaurant, café, concert hall and ballroom completed in 1911.

much of its time to the convivial occupations of eating and drinking in public. In Prague, digestion in one form or another seems to figure as importantly as it does in France.

I have to say that, on the whole, Czech food is unimaginative; even my favourite guidebook (written by loyal Praguers) concedes that "Czech cuisine is both nourishing and appetizing but requires a good digestion." The main course offered at most Prague restaurants today consists of a slab of roast meat—usually pork—fortified with boiled potatoes or dumplings (a Czech speciality), embellished with sauerkraut and irrigated by a thin gravy. Cooked green vegetables are not popular among Czechs and are rarely served; "green salad" almost always means sliced cucumber doused in the local cider vinegar.

You can, however, do much better than that if you know where to look; a tradition of fine cuisine—of wonderful soups, roasts, schnitzels, smoked meats, sausages and pastries comparable to those of Vienna—still survives, despite the uninspired uniformity that is inevitable when cooks and restaurateurs have become mere state employees.

The last place to look for good food is in the luxury hotels, which do provide "international" menus but at preposterous prices. The heartening thing about eating out in Prague is that—with one exception I have known—the best food is scarcely more expensive than the worst. The costly exception has been Prague's solitary Chinese restaurant, where the talented chef—remarkably, a Praguer—was taught the intricacies of oriental cuisine by professionals from Peking, until they were obliged to quit the city abruptly a few years ago, when the political climate between Czechoslovakia and China changed for the worse.

I've rarely enjoyed better fare—regardless of price—than is provided in an inexpensive restaurant near the Old Jewish Cemetery, in the Old Town, where *Rabínova kupsa* ("the rabbi's pocket")—pork stuffed with ham and cheese—is the favourite dish of the regular customers. The best food I've ever eaten in Prague, however, I found at a suburban restaurant some distance from the city centre, up the tram tracks towards Strašnice. There, you can enjoy one magnificent dish after another, such as *Husíjátru na cibulce* (goose liver and onions), *Kyjovské telecí medailonky zapečené* (gratin of veal medallions), or a spicy combination of meats known as *Stárkovská pochoutka* (master-brewer's delicatessen). The most expensive of these dishes costs scarcely more than one hour's wages for a skilled worker; and it will be accompanied by one of the excellent Czech wines, much underestimated by the world at large.

Generally speaking, good food is to be found in any Prague *vinárna*, or restaurant that serves wine. Mediocre food—or worse—is purveyed by the places where beer is the accompanying drink. Unfortunately, such places are the rule rather than the exception, for beer is the Czech national drink. The Bavarians occasionally consume slightly more, and the Belgians are sometimes sturdy runners-up; but, year after year, the Czechs are among the world's leaders in beer-drinking, disposing annually of more than 30 gallons of the stuff for every man, woman and child in the land.

Happiness in Prague, then, is a seat in a beer parlour with a glass of *pivo* (beer) in your fist; and I know few other places where the women drain their glasses with as much relish as the men. Some of the Czech beers—such as Prazdroj from Plzeň and Staropramen from Prague—have an international reputation. American tourists, on spotting bottled Budweiser in Prague, usually assume that it has been imported from Missouri. But they are wrong; this brand was being brewed in České Budějovice (Budweis in German) long before Anheuser-Busch of St. Louis started their expensive campaign to persuade the United States that "When you've said Budweiser, you've said it all."

In Prague alone there are four breweries to quench the city's great thirst; and I don't suppose anyone has ever tried to count the number of places in the city where their products are on tap. A classic Prague tavern can be found along any of the many arcaded streets in the old inner districts. Huge doors—that look medieval, even if some of them aren't—open on to stone steps that descend into a dimly lit barrel-vaulted cellar, furnished with long tables and benches or chairs.

The most famous tavern of all is down a side-street east of the river. Outside, an enormous clock in a wrought-iron case hangs over the pavement, announcing the name U Fleků (At Flek's), an abbreviation of the name of Jakub Flekovský, who gave the place its reputation after taking it over in 1762. It had, however, been slaking thirsts from at least as far back as the year 1499.

Since 1948, of course, U Fleků has been a publicly owned enterprise; but its reputation has endured, based upon a number of attractions. It has room for 900 customers at a time, who may find themselves seated either indoors or out in the beer garden, supping their *pivo* at long tables beneath the trees. In the summer months many of the patrons are tourists, especially from Germany, where U Fleků is far-famed. The tavern serves only its own beer—a heavy, rich black ale—which is brewed on the premises. You can only taste this special brew at U Fleků; all proddings to have it more widely distributed have been resisted by the managers, since it cannot be transported without loss of quality. The little brewery, in the yard alongside the beer garden, is operated by just three men. They use the good Prague water that springs up from two wells almost under their feet; the hops of Žatec in northern Bohemia; and four different kinds of malt. And they have nearly 500 years of tradition behind them.

More than 130,000 gallons of beer are consumed at U Fleků every year, which helps to explain its hearty atmosphere. In the evenings entertainments are staged in one of the rooms alongside the garden, with jugglers and soubrettes, and comedians who provoke gales of beery laughter from

In a basement nightclub near Wenceslas Square, some of Prague's numerous jazz fans enjoy a performance by an amateur band. The city has at least a dozen similar clubs, where patrons can drink, dance to popular music and, in some cases, watch cabaret well into the small hours.

the customers. Boisterous family parties, getting merrier by the minute, line the tables. The waiters thread their way dexterously through the bibulous throng, with trays full of brimming glasses balanced just above their shoulders. "*Na zdraví!*" the drinkers call to each other as they bump their glasses together and then drain them in a series of serpentine gulps. After visiting U Fleků one understands why so many Praguers are well-proportioned about the belt.

While the cabaret plays throughout the evening at old Jakub Flekovský's gold-mine, other night-spots in the city are doing good business too. The strains of jazz floating up from a cellar along Národní třída, one of central Prague's broad thoroughfares, mean that the Reduta Club is swinging tonight. The northern end of Wenceslas Square is always loud with music when the summer darkness falls, for the clubs there have their windows flung wide open. People in evening dress, returning from listening to the more delicate strains of Mozart at the 18th-Century neoclassical Tyl Theatre, wrinkle their noses at such robust sounds, but the cheerful din helps to relieve the boredom of the group of three or four policemen who generally are stationed across the tram tracks from one of the smart hotels. Presently, the last show ends at the numerous cinemas nearby and there is a final bustle of pedestrians along the square. The kerbside stalls that sell hot sausages on bread do their last business before closing down for the night. By 12 o'clock, Prague has become an almost deserted city, disturbed only by the swish of the water carts that wash down the streets and the intermittent rumble of the all-night trams.

If Praguers were polled about what they preferred to do when not at work, watching or taking part in sport would probably come at least as high on the list as it does in any other great city of the world. There are two excellent soccer teams in Prague—Dukla and Sparta—both of which have large and devout followings. They regularly enter the annual competition for the European Cup. Moto-cross meetings are held at weekends on the outskirts of the city. But the most popular spectator sport is undoubtedly ice hockey; and, of recent years, Prague has fallen into a particularly deep gloom whenever the Czech national team has been defeated by the arch-opponent, a Soviet side.

Among the more active pastimes—especially for young people—there is nothing to compare with gymnastics. As in other East European countries, there is unstinting investment of money, time and effort in grooming talented young solo gymnasts for gruelling international competition; but in Czechoslovakia there is also a strong tradition, dating from the 19th Century, of mass gymnastic displays.

Throughout the land, small children practise in the school gymnasium for hours each week with but one aim in view: to participate in the Spartakiade, a great national gymnastic display that takes place in Prague every five years. In a gigantic concrete stadium—the largest in the world—on the hill south-west of Prague Castle, 15,000 girls aged nine or 10 spend several days demonstrating complex balletic movements, and 15,000 small boys perform rather more athletic sequences. The older children then take over with further mass displays, set to specially composed music. The competition to select the music is held two years before the Spartakiade, so that the young athletes will have ample training time in which to become familiar with it. In all, some 150,000 performers appear over the course of each Spartakiade, which lasts for about a week and is popular enough to attract almost a quarter of a million spectators on each of the days of performances.

Besides being sporting enthusiasts, Praguers are also expert at the art of simple relaxation. Like all those who have to endure hard winters every year of their lives, they make the most of the sun when it appears. With an average temperature of −4°C (25°F), January and February invariably bring thick snow and ice to Prague, and everyone muffles up with a warm hat and high boots. In more clement seasons of the year, Praguers like especially to go for brisk walks in the parks and along the banks of the Vltava or, at weekends, in the surrounding countryside. But—although there is only a 20°C difference between the mean winter and summer temperatures—summer days can sometimes be very hot. At such times particularly, the 30 large parks throughout the city come into their own: people sprawl on the grass practically from dawn to dusk, even on weekdays, and eat a great deal of ice cream.

On hot days much bare flesh is exposed at the Barrandov open-air swimming pool, which has been carved out of the rock on the west bank of the Vltava. Even more is visible if you take one of the crowded pleasure

Taken out of the action by a mid-game collision, a Prague ice-hockey player watches helplessly as his opponent, from a visiting east Bohemian team, pirouettes in pursuit of the puck. Ice hockey is Czechoslovakia's favourite sport after soccer. The national team has on several occasions won the world championship.

steamers that travel the 25 miles upstream to Slapy, where the river has been dammed to form a vast artificial lake. It is Prague's substitute for the distant seaside; the nearest coast is 250 miles away in Poland. Slapy is a seasonal holiday resort but it attracts Praguers throughout the year as the weather dictates.

Whenever they have the time, the more mobile and affluent Praguers will set off for distant parts of the republic. A favourite destination is the Tatra Mountains of central Slovakia, where one can ski, hunt game, or just camp and relax amid wild scenery. But at weekends the typical Praguer heads for the nearer resorts with an ardour that has given rise to yet another of the city's dry jokes. It is said that the authorities, perturbed at the number of citizens who were abandoning work at lunchtime on Friday in order to make an early start, ordered the police to carry out spot checks of outward-bound afternoon traffic and to turn back the work-dodgers. "We soon got round that one," say the wily Praguers. "We started off on Thursday night instead."

Apart from Slapy, another popular destination is Karlštejn Castle, 23 miles south-west of the city. Standing high on a wooded crag above a narrow valley, the fortified castle was originally built between 1348 and 1355 for Charles IV by the French architect Matthew of Arras, and was completely restored in 1888 in the Gothic style. The unwarlike Charles originally used it as a country retreat and as a repository for imperial and royal jewellery and state archives; but it is a redoubtable piece of masonry that was able to survive a seven-month siege by Hussites in the 15th

Century and another long attack by an invading Swedish army a couple of hundred years later in the course of the Thirty Years' War.

Praguers go there to enjoy the spectacular views of the pine-forested slopes from the castle battlements and to marvel at the richly decorated chambers. Most gorgeous of these is the Chapel of the Holy Rood, sited under the roof of the highest tower. Its walls are encrusted with semi-precious stones, pieces of glass inlaid with gold hang from the ceiling and dozens of ikons bear witness to the faith that once flourished there. The visitors shuffle through in long lines, attentive to the guides rehearsing the history of Karlštejn. Then they plod slowly back down the valley, pausing—as like as not—for a refreshing *pivo* somewhere along the village street. Most will be back in Prague by nightfall.

But the luckiest weekenders usually forgo sightseeing to make for a place of their own in the countryside. Some very prosperous citizens—high-ranking Party members, for example—may have *chalupas*, which can be quite large places; many of them are farmhouses that once belonged to German families who were evicted from Czechoslovakia in the immediate post-war period. But most weekend cottages are no more than *chatas*, which are much smaller; most of those I've seen are simple wooden constructions, like ridge-tents made of timber, with the two long sides rising to an apex and the ends closed with wooden walls. There are said to be 100,000 of them within a 60-mile radius of Prague. Certainly, they are an ambition—practically a cult—of every family in the city. Tuzex obligingly supplies prefabricated structures for as little as 2,950 of its coupons—worth about 15,000 Czech crowns, or between four and six months' pay for the average wage-earner—and there is a section in its catalogue significantly entitled "Equipment for handymen *and cottage owners*", clearly aimed at customers who have a *chata* or a *chalupa* among their resources. Very often *chatas* are entirely home-made from any timber the owner can lay his hands on; you sometimes see them standing in little rows upon plots of leased ground beside country roads.

Because of their small size and primitive facilities, the *chatas* can be nothing more than occasional retreats; and their occupants must be prepared to put up with only modest comfort, spending as much time as possible in the open air. Their chief value, I think, is as a psychological release from the tensions inseparable from living in any city—but especially Prague, which brings its own peculiar pressures to bear on its citizens.

One of the worst is the severe lack of living space in the city. Although, compared with the large-scale urbanization seen elsewhere during the 20th Century, Prague's post-war population growth has been small—perhaps a quarter of a million—the housing supply has signally failed to keep up either with the modest increase in numbers or with people's expectations of a rise in the standard of living. In addition, the public ownership of almost all property in Prague makes it difficult for most people to take steps to provide themselves with a home by their own efforts. A fortunate minority of Praguers—for example those who are in well-paid occupations or those whose employers will make them a loan for the purpose—have the opportunity to buy their own small house or flat, at a cost that is roughly eight times the national average yearly wage; but most citizens must rely upon rented accommodation provided by the municipality. There is simply not enough; during the 1960s and 1970s, it was not unusual for Praguers to have to wait 10 or even 15 years to be rehoused—although this period can be greatly reduced for those with the right influence and qualifications, such as being employed in a government post or in an industrial or technical job that is highly valued by the Party. And because of the labour shortage in the construction industry, the authorities freely admit that the situation is unlikely to improve materially before the end of the century.

As a result, three generations are sometimes obliged to live together; and divorced couples may have to share the same roof even after their official separation. There are strict regulations about the number of square feet of floor space each individual is allowed; if a member of a family dies or leaves home, the family is no longer eligible for its previous amount of space, and must find someone to register as living with them, or move to a smaller house or flat. It is from such cramped and oppressive conditions that the weekend *chata* offers a doubly welcome escape.

The *chata* is also a place where the Praguer can feel—for a couple of days a week at least—that he is his own master, and where he will not be constantly made aware, even by such little reminders as the sight of a police car, that authority hems him in.

The manifestations of Czechoslovakia's authoritarian regime are seldom overt. To me, there seem to be fewer policemen on the streets than there are, say, in the United States. True, Czech police wear pistols at their belts—but that seems to be the custom in every country except Britain. And, apart from their red hatbands and epaulettes, they are indistinguishable from khaki clad soldiers—but, again, there are other nations in the world where the constabulary is intentionally kitted out to look like a paramilitary force. The only Prague cops I've ever had dealings with—including one who stopped my Czech taxi-driver for speeding—have always been perfectly correct and usually very polite, not at all menacing or ugly; and that is more than can be said for some of the other police forces I've encountered around the world.

Only the most observant visitor will be mindful from what he sees that Czechoslovakia is an occupied country. The Kremlin has wished the rest of the world to believe that, once "normalization" was achieved during the 12 months or so following August 1968, Soviet troops went home and left the Czechs to keep their own house in order. Not so; some 70,000

Soviet soldiers remain in the country. There is a barracks full of them a little way up the tram tracks behind Prague Castle, and its occupants are under the strictest instructions never to leave the building except in civilian dress, for fear of offending the Czech citizens. (However, most Praguers can spot a Soviet private at 50 yards, even when he is not in uniform. So, when one of these young men goes into town for a beer, he generally has to wait a very long time before he is served.) Nevertheless, they are there. As the Praguers say, in another of their topical quips: "We are the most non-aligned nation in the world today. Why, we don't even interfere in the internal affairs of our own country any more."

From time to time since 1968, citizens who do not like the present state of affairs have subtly let their feelings show, sometimes in the drollest of ways. There was the occasion a few years ago when a number of shops in Prague apparently began to demonstrate spontaneously the most zealous support for the "alliance" with the Soviet Union. Huge portraits appeared in their windows depicting Lenin, Leonid Brezhnev and Gustáv Husák, who had supplanted Alexander Dubček as leader of the Czech Communist Party, and later became President. Some time after these displays had begun to proliferate, the authorities realized that almost all of them were in shops belonging to either butchers or hairdressers. Invariably, President Brezhnev would be situated between a couple of pigs' heads in the butcher's window, while the image of the dazzlingly bald Lenin was flanked at the barber's by a pair of shaggy-haired dummies. In both locations President Husák's photograph would be carefully placed at the bottom of the display, in a position suggesting his inferior status to that of the Russians. The word eventually came down from on high that this sort of thing must stop, and of course it did.

The strongest act of dissent since 1968 has had much nastier repercussions. Early one morning during my last visit to Prague I walked round a corner in Malá Strana and saw, chalked on a wall facing me, the inscription CHARTA 77. Three hours later, when I returned the same way, the inscription had disappeared, rubbed out by authority or perhaps by a non-sympathizer—who knows? But for a short time that day, passers-by had been reminded that many citizens of Czechoslovakia bitterly resent the authoritarian rule of their present government.

The Charter of 1977 to which the inscription referred was a document circulated in Prague that year, criticizing the government's failure to observe certain basic human rights in Czechoslovakia. It specifically drew attention to the fact that these rights were not only written into the Czech Constitution but had also been internationally ratified, amid great hullabaloo, by governments of both the East and the West at the Helsinki Conference held in 1975.

The Helsinki agreement had stated, for example, that all countries should allow foreign newspapers to be available to those of their citizens

Spring sunshine lures Praguers outside to sunbathe on one of several jetties, erected for swimmers, along the banks of the Vltava. Downstream, near the Svatopluk Čech Bridge, boating fans amuse themselves in hired skiffs. In summer, the river becomes Prague's most popular outdoor playground.

who wished to buy them. As the authors of Charter '77 pointed out, this has not happened. News-stands do carry papers from the Soviet Union, the German Democratic Republic and other parts of Eastern Europe; but the *New York Times*, *The Guardian*, *Le Monde* and other reputable non-Communist publications from the West are still forbidden to the Czech with an interest in international affairs. Nor is any domestic newspaper or journal allowed to publish matter critical of the government. *Literární listy*, that best-selling organ of the Writers' Union in the Dubček days, was one of the first victims of "normalization" and has long since vanished from the streets of the capital.

Another article of the Helsinki agreement stipulated that people should be allowed to move freely between one country and another, if they wished. But for Czechs who cannot demonstrate a long loyalty to the Communist Party it remains very difficult to obtain permission to take a foreign holiday outside the Communist bloc. When a non-Party member does get such permission, the authorities usually make sure that at least one close member of his family stays behind, just in case the traveller takes it into his head not to return.

Charter '77 dissented from methods such as these—and therefore those who subscribed to it were by definition "dissidents". They were a medley of idealistic people including both anti-Communists and those who had associated themselves with the reformist Communism of the previous decade and who preferred to stay behind after the Soviet invasion in order to resume the struggle for reform, rather than emigrate while the going was good; as a result, they have been systematically persecuted.

Every Praguer you meet can count off on his fingers the number of his old friends who made that quick decision to leave in 1968. Vienna was usually the first stop. The Austrian capital is only 30 miles from Czechoslovakia's southern frontier. From Vienna the emigrants spread themselves across the Old and New Worlds, just as their forefathers had done for centuries when circumstances at home had become uncomfortable—or worse. Only a few have since returned, having come to terms with a government that has been careful not to exact a bitter price for their brief disloyalty. But most of them have stayed away, knowing that they would probably never be able to resume their earlier way of life. Some have been tried in their absence for the "illegal" act of departing and failing to return; others have been able to regularize their residence abroad by paying the Czech authorities huge sums of money as a recompense for the State's investment in their education and upbringing, so that they may receive visits from their families, or return themselves should they wish to do so at some future date.

From time to time word filters through from the self-imposed exiles in Montreal, London, Cape Town, Cologne, Detroit. They report that all is well with them; but they seem hungry for every scrap of news from Prague.

And the ones who stayed behind sometimes seem to dwell too long upon this pining for home. This or that relative or friend, they say, is doing well—but then they quickly switch to an elaborate description of the homesickness that he or she must be feeling. Before long, they are saying "Things aren't so bad here, you know", and enumerating the good things about life in Prague—the excellent beer, the improvements in living standards, the beauty of the city and of the countryside.

These stay-behinds generally keep their own counsel where politics are concerned, for they belong to a people who have discovered painfully since 1968 that trust is in short supply and that too many men have their price. Perhaps the most terrible thing about life in Prague today is the fact that even close friends will avoid mentioning such dangerous topics as Charter '77 in each other's company.

In the meantime life goes on, and the local television service just about sums up its curious texture. The programmes can be brilliantly sustaining, particularly when they deal with national culture or sport. But for too many hours of the week there is nothing available but grey, turgid discussions of various socialist texts and excessively strident reports about the opening or progress of some unimportant public enterprise. Better by far to seek your pleasure elsewhere—and most Praguers do.

Young intellectuals still sit in the Viola coffee-house as they did in 1968, but the conversation now concerns literature and art in their less pointedly relevant forms. Otherwise, Praguers get on with making as much money as they can and with keeping out of harm's way. They comfort themselves with the thought that, whatever the doldrums of the working week, Friday and (with luck) the *chata* beckon every seven days.

The Playground at Slapy

Houseboats are beached or moored on the strand fringing the peninsula of Ždán, a popular spot on Slapy lake, where cottages and cabins nestle among trees.

Getting away from it all is a way of life for Praguers, whose weekday living conditions are often cramped by the city's chronic housing shortage. Czechoslovakia has no sea coast, so a favourite destination for weekenders is the artificial lake of Slapy, an hour's drive from the city, where a hydroelectric dam across the Vltava River has created a 25-square-mile stretch of protected water, bordered by steep hillsides and beaches of specially imported sand. Dotted over the slopes are the second homes that most Prague families aspire to, ranging from modest wooden shacks built by the owners to converted old stone farmhouses. Scores of houseboats line the lakeside; campers pitch their tents in the woods; and day-trippers—many of whom make the 25-mile journey by pleasure steamer up the river—come to picnic and sunbathe.

A windsurfer enjoys one of Slapy's most popular watersports. Behind him, holiday homes perched precariously on the rock face have a fine view of the lake.

Two-bunk huts (left) built by the government in the woods near the lake are used as summer campsites by the Czechoslovak Army and youth groups such as the Pioneers—the junior arm of the Socialist Youth Union. The modern tents (inset) are pitched by families on every inch of available space along the waterfront.

An angler hopefully casts his line from the lake shore. Carp of all sizes, pike, perch and tench can be caught in Slapy's tranquil stretch of fresh water.

Clad in a two-piece swimsuit for maximum exposure to sun, an elderly but energetic holiday-maker on a country walk strides along to keep up with her dog.

A man sunbathes placidly while his daughter tries a somersault on his back. Country weekends are very popular among Praguers with young families.

A well-to-do couple stand proudly beside their handsomely appointed houseboat at its lakeside mooring. Slapy has some 2,000 of these floating homes—all confined permanently to the shore. Anti-pollution regulations, introduced in 1977, forbid the movement of motorized craft on the lake, except in designated water-skiing areas.

The lucky owner of a holiday log cabin relaxes over lunch on his veranda, with its view of trees and neat garden plot. One of the more luxurious second homes erected at Slapy, this chalet was built by the owner from a packaged, do-it-yourself kit; it boasts a comfortably furnished living room and modern fittings in the kitchen (above). Smaller chalets are often much more basic, some even without running water.

Three friends enjoy the pleasures of relaxed conversation after a meal in this picnic area on a Slapy hillside. The privacy and peace they find here is a welcome antidote to the weekday tensions of life in the overcrowded capital.

3

A Millennium of Changing Fortunes

The Vltava is not one of the great rivers of Europe, but its passage through Prague makes it one of the most memorable. It rises among the forest-clad mountains of southern Bohemia and rushes swiftly northward, negotiating rapids and gorges, for 250 miles before it reaches the capital; there, its shallow waters—by now a quarter of a mile wide—describe a huge curve that is punctuated by eight small islands and spanned by a total of 13 bridges. Continuing northward, the river becomes deeper and more tranquil and, after 18 miles, flows by the old town of Mělník, set among hillside vineyards where a celebrated white wine is made. At Mělník, the Vltava mingles with the River Elbe (known to the Czechs as the Labe), which thereafter rolls mightily across northern Europe, carrying a busy commerce as far as Hamburg and the North Sea.

Each day, some of that commerce returns upstream to the Vltava and to Prague. Amid the noisy factories on the city's outskirts you can often see snub-nosed, shallow-draught barges swinging into riverside wharfs, their diesel engines throbbing. But, for most Praguers, the Vltava is principally a playground. Pleasure cruisers packed with sightseers ply between the city centre and Prague's spacious zoo in the northern suburbs. Youngsters in frail dinghies and canoes flirt dangerously with the torrent of water over the Vltava's weirs. And everywhere there are the anglers. In rows along the banks, or in little boats anchored in midstream, they crouch for hours over their rods, eyes patiently fixed upon the waters where carp and pike swim.

The Vltava divides Prague into almost equal halves, which explains why there are so many bridges to cross: most of them carry a ceaseless stream of tramcars and motor vehicles that rattle and rumble all day long between the east and west banks. But traffic is banned from Prague's oldest and most beautiful span, the 560-yard Charles Bridge, which joins the Old Town and Malá Strana. Built in the 14th Century to replace an earlier crossing destroyed by floods, the Charles Bridge is defended at both ends by massive Gothic gate-towers with pointed roofs, and rests upon 15 sandstone piers; on the upstream side, huge ramps of tree trunks protect the piers from damage by the ice that floats down the Vltava in winter.

Had it remained as its medieval builders designed it, the Charles Bridge would have been a handsome enough structure; but from the 17th Century onwards, Roman Catholic monks, nobility and officials—inhabiting a Prague ruled by the conquering Habsburgs—erected at regular intervals along both its parapets 30 statues of Christian saints; and it is these additions that make the bridge one of the most remarkable in Europe. The

Rebelling against the rule of the Catholic Holy Roman Empire, Protestant Bohemian nobles —shown here in a contemporary engraving— attempt to assassinate officials of the Habsburg Emperor by hurling them from the upper-storey windows of Prague Castle on May 23, 1618. But the victims survived their "Defenestration", and the Czech rebels, crushed by Habsburg armies in 1620, remained a subject people for 300 years.

stone saints, many of whom lift their hands in gestures of benediction, are uniformly baroque in style, even though the newest of them was placed in position as recently as 1928. Through their grimy patina of age and dirt, many of the statues gleam with recent touches of gold paint—applied to a halo here, to a brandished crucifix there.

The Charles Bridge is always thronged with pedestrians. Some are simply going about their business, striding purposefully from one side of the river to the other. But the majority dawdle across, enjoying the sights around them. Artists will sketch your portrait there. Lovers can lean closely together against the parapet and dreamily watch the Vltava flowing below. Almost everyone lingers over the magnificent view of Prague Castle and St. Vitus' Cathedral rising above Malá Strana and the western bridge-tower. But thoughtful Praguers must often contemplate the Charles Bridge itself and remember how much of their city's history has passed over it.

The bridge takes its name from Charles IV, King of Bohemia and Holy Roman Emperor, who had it built in the late 1350s as part of his effort to transform Prague into the greatest city in northern Europe. Charles was born in Prague in 1316, son and heir of John of Luxembourg, whom the Czech nobility had six years earlier chosen as their King after he had married Eliška, last survivor of the native Přemyslid dynasty. Unfortunately, John turned out to be an absentee monarch who spent most of his reign fighting all over Europe, from Italy to Lithuania (where he was blinded). He only returned to Prague in order to extort from his luckless subjects yet more money to pay for his wars. France was John's favourite country and it was to the French court that he sent his son to be educated when Charles was only seven; the boy's tutor was Pierre Roger, the French abbot who later became Pope Clement VI.

When Charles returned to Prague 10 years later, a sophisticated and cosmopolitan prince, his father made him Margrave (military governor) of Moravia and, in effect, Regent of Bohemia. As he grew to manhood, Charles shared in the defence of his family's scattered European possessions by campaigning in Poland, Austria and, above all, the northern Italian states—where he was profoundly affected by early Humanist thinkers, such as Petrarch, and their enlightened views on government and society. His fighting came to an end in 1346 on the battlefield of Crécy, when King John—a long-time ally of the French monarch—led an impetuous cavalry charge against the English army and fell, mortally wounded, under a hail of English arrows. Charles was proclaimed King of Bohemia; from then on, he rarely went to war and earned in more constructive ways his reputation as one of medieval Europe's greatest rulers.

By chance, Charles had been elected Holy Roman Emperor a few months before he was even a king, thanks to the support of his ex-tutor, who was by now Pope. The Holy Roman Empire—a confederation of

In the Chapel of St. Wenceslas within St. Vitus' Cathedral, a spotlight illuminates a figure of Wenceslas, patron saint of Bohemia and founder of the original cathedral. The cult of St. Wenceslas—historically a 10th-Century ruler noted for his piety, but represented in this Gothic statue as the perfect knight of medieval chivalry—was introduced in the 14th Century by one of Bohemia's greatest kings, Charles IV.

kingdoms, principalities, bishoprics and cities under the overall authority of an emperor who claimed to be the successor of the Caesars—was medieval Europe's most powerful political unit; at this period it stretched from Hungary in the east to France in the west, and from Rome in the south to Denmark in the north. The office of emperor, the secular leader of Western European Christianity, has been described as that of "Christendom's professional bully", but Charles IV always preferred diplomacy to force. His most enlightened imperial act was to issue a decree known as the "Golden Bull" (so called because its *bulla*, or seal, was of gold), which created order out of the chaos that had long surrounded the election of an emperor.

But, throughout his career, Charles's first concern was always for his native land of Bohemia. In the *Vita Caroli*, his autobiography in Latin, the new King describes the legacy he has inherited from his spendthrift father: "We found that kingdom so ravaged that there was not one free castle that was not mortgaged, together with all the royal possessions. We had nowhere to reside except city houses, just like any burgher." Fortunately, there was nothing fundamentally wrong with Bohemia's economy. The royal coffers happened to be empty because citizens had hitherto been reluctant to pay taxes to a king who squandered them on foreign wars. The national coinage, the silver groschen, was, in fact, one of the hardest currencies in Europe, thanks to its consistently high precious metal content —the result of the rich silver lodes that had been mined since the 13th Century at Kutná Hora and Jihlava, two towns south-east of Prague.

Charles immediately set about reviving his kingdom's prosperity. He resumed the collection of taxes, invited German merchants to settle in Bohemia's towns, and made the roads safe for trade by clearing them of robbers and repairing their surfaces. He commissioned numerous churches, monasteries, hospitals and castles, shrewdly realizing that such large-scale building activity would stimulate the economy and, at the same time, alleviate unemployment among his subjects.

The King also took a great interest in Bohemia's agriculture. He introduced fish-ponds all over the country and ordered them to be stocked with carp (still the traditional Christmas dish of the Czechs). He encouraged sheep farming so that his people could trade in wool—a major commodity in medieval Europe—and in 1358 one of his decrees brought the grapevine to Mělník, together with French experts to advise upon the best methods of cultivation. In only one sphere were Charles's reforms unsuccessful. He drew up the *Majestas Carolina*, a codification of traditional Bohemian law; but this so incensed the country's turbulent nobility—who had grown accustomed, under King John's negligent rule, to making their own laws—that Charles was obliged to withdraw the document.

Central to Charles's ambitions was the regeneration of Prague, the city of his birth. In 1348 he founded there the Charles University, the first in central Europe; in the foundation charter, the King expressed a wish that

In this delicately coloured woodcut dating from 1493—the earliest known view of Prague—the jagged silhouettes of St. Vitus' Cathedral and Prague Castle along the ridge of Hradčany (background) dominate the skyline as they do to this day. Below the castle hill, the walled settlement of Malá Strana (centre) is linked by the Charles Bridge to the Old Town (right).

his new university should contain "a large number of learned men, so that loyal inhabitants of the Kingdom need not go abroad to beg for help, but may find a table spread for a banquet within the Kingdom". Charles's brainchild grew into one of the most influential institutions in Prague, not least because of its great size; during its early years it was said to have 7,000 students, in a town of no more than 40,000 inhabitants. Scholars flocked there from Germany, Poland, France, Italy and England, attracted by the high standard of teaching. Yet, in spite of the university's international character, it quickly became the ideological centre of Czech nationalism, a force that was soon to have a profound effect on life in Bohemia.

On the east bank of the Vltava, Charles built a New Town (Nové Město) to the south of the Old Town; and on its west bank, he enclosed Malá Strana and Hradčany with a stout wall. He brought skilled architects from abroad, including the Frenchman Matthew of Arras, who began to rebuild the Cathedral of St. Vitus on the heights of Hradčany, and the German Peter Parler, who designed the Charles Bridge and continued Matthew's work on the cathedral. Once again, these enterprises were partly intended as public works projects; to this day, the stretch of fortifications that Charles had erected on Petřín Hill, south of Prague Castle, is known as the "Hunger Wall". In order to give his restored capital a good start, the King freed it from all taxes for nearly 20 years in all and stipulated that

foreign traders who entered his kingdom should first display their merchandise in Prague, so that its citizens could pick the choicest items.

It is difficult to avoid the conclusion that Charles IV was one of the most civilized monarchs who ever lived. In addition to his genius for practical government, he was an extremely tolerant man. Although he was Holy Roman Emperor—and the friend of a Pope who had been a Benedictine abbot—he invited the reforming preacher Conrad of Waldhauser to become parish priest of the Týn Church in Prague's Old Town Square, in spite of that cleric's inflammatory sermons attacking the indolence and immorality of the religious orders.

In short, Charles was everything his father had not been: a considerate man and a careful king. He lost three wives in succession but bore their premature deaths philosophically; and his contemporaries often spoke of his meek, pious demeanour. Charles was 62 when he died in 1378—an old man by the standards of the Middle Ages—and his last words to his eldest son were: "Love friends, not money. Money will never make you the supreme lord of Christendom."

At the age of 17, that son duly became Wenceslas IV, King of Bohemia and Holy Roman Emperor. His capital, Prague, was by now one of the most splendid cities of Europe: its political life was stable, its trade was flourishing, its great university attracted scholars from all over the Continent, and its magnificent Gothic architecture inspired all who saw it.

Most of these benefits could be directly ascribed to Charles IV's wise rule—although the Czechs had also been lucky in that the Black Death, the plague that repeatedly ravaged Europe in the 14th Century, had largely spared Bohemia. But the reign of Wenceslas was to see the end of the kingdom's peace and prosperity. The new King shared his father's love of Prague and distaste for foreign adventures; however, unlike Charles, Wenceslas also thoroughly disliked the business of government. His favourite occupations appear to have been hunting, drinking and roaming the streets of Prague at night in disguise, accompanied by a band of unruly companions. He was not the man to cope with the deep divisions that soon became apparent within Bohemian society.

By the late 14th Century, German merchants, attracted by Bohemia's booming economy, had settled in large numbers in the towns of the kingdom and in many of them—such as the Old Town of Prague—they had come to control the municipal council. Czech resentment at this alien infiltration was only equalled by their suspicion of the Church, which owned almost half of Bohemia's land, yet owed allegiance to a Pope in Rome. In addition, the Church's use of the Latin language did not commend itself to a Slav nation. Wenceslas half-heartedly attempted to placate Czech nationalist feeling by insisting that the Old Town administration and the Charles University should come under Czech rather than German control. From the German-speaking lands that all but surrounded Bohemia

From Tribes to Dynasties

A.D. c. 400-600 Slav migrants from Dniepr River marshlands colonize area of present-day Czechoslovakia. Tribe known as Čechy (Czechs) settles in regions of Bohemia and Moravia; Slovaks occupy Slovakia

c. 830 Rise of Great Moravian Empire, a confederation of Slav peoples organized for mutual trade and defence

c. 850 Construction of fortresses on hills of Hradčany and Vyšehrad marks foundation of Prague, which becomes the seat of the Přemyslids, the ruling Czech dynasty. Byzantine missionaries, Cyril and Methodius, set about converting Great Moravia to Christianity

c. 907 Magyar invaders from Hungary destroy Moravian Empire (Slovakia to remain Hungarian possession for a thousand years); but Czechs retain independence by allying with neighbouring German kingdom

928 Henry, King of the Germans, exacts tribute from Prince Václav of Bohemia—the "Good King Wenceslas" of the carol

962 Otto, son of Henry, is crowned Emperor of the Holy Roman Empire (Bohemia to stay within its orbit for 450 years)

11th Century German traders, attracted by underpopulated Slav lands, settle on the east bank of the Vltava, thus forming the nucleus of the Old Town district

1198 Holy Roman Emperor Philip of Swabia grants in perpetuity to Prince Přemysl Otakar I and his heirs the title of King of Bohemia

c. 1235 King Václav I grants Old Town status of an independent borough and right to erect walls

1257 Malá Strana (Lesser Quarter) founded near the walls of Prague Castle

1270 Prague's large Jewish community builds Old-New Synagogue, oldest surviving synagogue in Europe

1306 Death of Václav III without heir extinguishes Přemyslid dynasty; John of Luxembourg, Václav's brother-in-law, succeeds

1344 Work begins on Cathedral of St. Vitus, initially under the French architect Matthew of Arras

1346-78 During the 32-year reign of Charles IV, King of Bohemia and Holy Roman Emperor, Prague becomes Empire's capital. New Town (Nové Město) is established and Charles University founded

1357 Construction of Charles Bridge, linking Malá Strana and Old Town, begins

1390s During reign of Charles's son, Wenceslas IV, Czech religious reformer Jan Hus preaches against ecclesiastical abuses. Hus attracts support from nationalistic Czechs and antagonizes conservative Czech and German inhabitants of Bohemia

1415 Hus is found guilty of heresy by the Council of Constance and is burnt at the stake

1419 First "Defenestration of Prague" occurs when rebellious followers of Hus storm New Town Hall and hurl pro-papal councillors from upper windows; incident sparks off the Hussite Wars, a fierce struggle between Czech reformers and Emperor Sigismund, who claims Bohemian throne after the death of his brother, Wenceslas IV

1420 Jan Žižka, leader of radical Hussite sect known as the Taborites, defeats imperial army led by Sigismund at Vítkov, east of Prague

1431 Last of Sigismund's several invasion attempts repulsed by Hussites near Domažlice in Bohemia

1434 At Battle of Lipany, in eastern Slovakia, moderate Hussites join with pro-papal Czechs to defeat Taborites, thus ending Hussite Wars

1436 Sigismund crowned King of Bohemia in Prague, but his death the following year ends Luxembourg dynasty; title of Emperor passes to the Austrian, Albert of Habsburg

1458 Election of George of Poděbrady, a Czech Hussite nobleman, to throne of Bohemia ends period of near-anarchy caused by disputed succession

1471 Death of King George; Bohemian throne passes to Catholic kings of the Polish Jagiełło dynasty

1526 Protestant Czech nobility elect Ferdinand of Habsburg King of Bohemia on condition that religious freedom is guaranteed

1541 Fire destroys Malá Strana and part of Hradčany; both rebuilt with splendid Renaissance buildings

1584-1612	Holy Roman Emperor Rudolf II moves his court to Prague, where he patronizes scientists and artists
1600	Population of Prague reaches 60,000
1618	Bohemian nobles, protesting against oppressive foreign rule, throw Habsburg officials from window of Prague Castle; this second "Defenestration" signals a revolt in Bohemia that embroils most of Europe in the Thirty Years' War
1620	Habsburg troops defeat Czech rebels at Battle of the White Mountain, outside Prague. During ensuing years, Protestant religion is proscribed in Bohemia and many Czechs emigrate. City is reduced to status of a provincial town within the Habsburg Empire
1648	Treaty of Westphalia ends Thirty Years' War
1703	Construction of St. Nicholas' Church in Malá Strana begins; finest of the many churches and monasteries built throughout this period by Catholics
1780-90	During enlightened reign of Austrian Emperor Josef II, religious freedom is granted to Bohemia. Introduction of secular education revives interest in Czech language and stimulates national feeling
1784	Prague's four townships—Malá Strana, Hradčany, Old Town and New Town—united into single city
1787	Mozart, in Prague, conducts first performance of his opera "Don Giovanni"
1817	City expands to include Karlín, its first planned industrial suburb
1837	Population climbs to more than 100,000
1848	Praguers rise in revolt and demand withdrawal of Austrian garrison; insurrection is quashed and absolutist rule more rigorously imposed
1860	New Constitution for Habsburg Empire confirms political dominance of Germans in Bohemia—who form only one-third of population
1862	Sokol Movement founded in Prague to promote gymnastics, but rapidly grows into powerful nationalist organization
1881	Inauguration of Prague's National Theatre
1914	Outbreak of First World War: Austria allies itself with Germany; Czechs and Slovaks conscripted into Austrian army. Czech nationalist leaders Tomáš Masaryk and Edvard Beneš flee to Paris to work for Czechoslovak independence
1918	War brings collapse of Austro-Hungarian Empire; independent Republic of Czechoslovakia proclaimed, with Masaryk as first President
1922	Greater Prague formed by the incorporation of more than 35 outlying industrial districts and villages
1937	City's population reaches an estimated 945,000
1938	Munich agreement between Germany, Italy, France and Britain, forces Czechs to cede to Germany the predominantly German-inhabited Sudetenland. Further territory ceded to Hungary and Poland reduces Czechoslovakia's area and population by a third
1939	President Beneš goes into exile in London. German troops occupy city; Bohemia and Moravia made a "Protectorate" of the Third Reich, while Slovakia becomes a puppet state under German protection
1942	Nazi administrator of Bohemia and Moravia, Reinhardt Heydrich, assassinated by Czech commandos. Nazis take savage reprisals including destruction of village of Lidice, near Prague
1945	Soviet troops liberate Prague. Beneš returns to form government in coalition with Communists
1948	Communist Party seizes power in Czechoslovakia
1952	Eleven leading Communists executed on charges of "revisionism" after show trial in Prague
1968	Alexander Dubček becomes Party leader and attempts to introduce more liberal style of Communism; but Soviet Union invades Czechoslovakia to re-establish status quo. Gustáv Husák succeeds Dubček as Party leader and later becomes President also
1975	Helsinki agreement guaranteeing human rights ratified by 35 countries of Eastern and Western blocs, including Czechoslovakia
1977	Charter '77, a manifesto signed by a thousand Czech citizens, criticizes their government's violation of Helsinki accords
1979	Playwright Václav Havel and four other signatories of Charter '77 imprisoned for dissident activity

the response was a violent protest against what were increasingly seen as the "heretical" tendencies of the independently minded Czech clergy.

The most prominent member of this latter group was Jan Hus. Born about 1373 into a peasant family of southern Bohemia, Hus studied at the Charles University and in 1396 became a philosophy lecturer there. His fellow-teachers had been much influenced by the writings of John Wycliffe, the English religious reformer—often called the "Morning Star of the Reformation"—who died in 1384, almost a century and a half before Martin Luther sparked off the Protestant revolution in Europe. A stern critic of the Church, Wycliffe castigated the corruption and worldliness of both the papacy and the lesser clergy, and questioned the validity of such cherished practices as the veneration of saints and the sale of indulgences (remissions of punishment for sin). He also urged that the Bible be translated from Latin into the vernacular in order to make it accessible to ordinary Christians. To the Czechs, who saw the church hierarchy and the German-speaking colonists as twin threats to their nation's political autonomy and to Slav culture, Wycliffe's words had a powerful appeal.

Hus himself soon had the opportunity to try out the Englishman's views on a wider audience. In 1402 he was appointed Rector of the Bethlehem Chapel, an austere, barn-like building recently erected just within the Old Town's southern walls to provide preaching in Czech—and Czech only—for a congregation of up to 3,000 people. (The chapel later fell into disuse and was largely demolished in the 18th Century; the building that stands on its site today is a faithful reconstruction, completed in 1954.)

While at the Bethlehem Chapel, Hus began a reform of the Czech language, in order to transform it from a mere spoken vernacular into a useful literary medium. He introduced the diacritical marks ˇ ´ and ° to replace clumsy combinations of letters; so that, for example, the word for "line", previously spelt czaara henceforth became čára. Czech as it is written today is largely Hus's handiwork. But it was his spirited preaching against current ecclesiastical abuses that made the greater impact on the inhabitants of 15th-Century Prague.

Before long, complaints about Hus began to pour in from the church authorities: that he had been criticizing the morals of the clergy; that he had been stirring up enmity between Czechs and Germans (to which he replied "A good German is dearer to me than a bad Czech"). Hus defiantly continued to attack the Church—then entering the Great Schism, a confused episode when three Popes ruled at one and the same time—and in 1409 he was even elected Rector of the Charles University. Archbishop Zbyněk of Prague retaliated by having 200 of Wycliffe's books publicly burned in the courtyard of the archiepiscopal palace and by having Hus excommunicated. Hus and his followers successfully defended the English reformer's reputation in a month-long "disputation"—an elaborate intellectual tournament common in the Middle Ages—and after

Enjoying late-autumn sunlight on the Charles Bridge, a crowd of strollers gathers to watch a painter sketch the view towards Prague Castle and the cathedral.

A Living Monument

For six centuries the people of Prague have been crossing and recrossing the sturdy, stone-built Charles Bridge, begun in the mid-14th Century to link the two halves of the city. Over the years the bridge has also served as a market-place, as a site for tournaments, and even—during a siege in the 17th Century—as a battlefield. Twelve other bridges now carry the city's traffic across the Vltava, and in 1965 the Charles Bridge was closed to motor vehicles. Today, it is a paradise for strollers, who can enjoy unrivalled views of the city and marvel as well at the bridge's own great attractions—the 30 magnificent statues of saints that form a spectacular open-air exhibition of baroque art.

A woman leads two of her dogs over the bridge, while a third travels in style.

A family group pauses by the bridge's parapet for a view of the Vltava.

A troupe of buskers provides impromptu entertainment for passing Praguers.

The base of a statue makes a convenient easel for an artist drawing the view.

it was over the students made up ribald songs about the Archbishop that were soon being chanted by ordinary citizens in the streets of Prague.

By now, Bohemia was divided into two fiercely opposed camps: the German and Czech supporters of the papacy versus the mainly Czech supporters of Hus. The vacillating Wenceslas still backed Hus—to the extent of forcing Archbishop Zbyněk to indemnify the owners of books that the cleric had had destroyed—but the King's frail resolution soon failed.

In 1411, one of the ruling Popes proclaimed a crusade against the King of Naples, who supported a rival, and decreed that the campaign should be financed by the selling of indulgences to faithful Catholics throughout Europe. Hus openly denounced this means of raising money; and when three young Praguers who had tried to obstruct the indulgence vendors were jailed, at the city magistrates' behest, in the Old Town Hall and then beheaded, riots broke out all over the city. Hus had the bodies taken to the Bethlehem Chapel, where he conducted a Martyrs' Mass before a huge congregation. But the frightened Wenceslas, anxious to reconcile the opposing parties, begged Hus to leave Prague. So the reformer continued his activities in the Bohemian countryside, where he often preached in the open fields to large crowds of peasants.

Hus re-emerged in 1414 in order to clear his name in person at the Church Council that had been convened at the German town of Constance (chiefly to end the Great Schism by choosing a Pope acceptable to all). He was given a safe-conduct by no less a person than Sigismund, Wenceslas' brother and heir, who was by now Holy Roman Emperor. The safe-conduct proved worthless; shortly after he reached Constance, Hus was imprisoned on the orders of papal officials, and for six months was brought from his dungeon repeatedly to face a panel of ecclesiastical judges and to answer the dozens of charges against him. These ranged from incitement against the clergy to criticism of the sacrament of the Mass, for Hus had argued that communicants should be given not only the consecrated wafer, as in accepted church practice, but also the chalice of wine, as at the Last Supper.

Hus steadfastly refused to recant and, on July 6, 1415, in a meadow outside Constance, he was burned at the stake. His ashes were thrown into the Rhine and all his possessions were destroyed, so that the Czechs should not have any relics of their martyr.

It is surprising that civil war did not break out at once in Bohemia. Prague was in uproar at the news of Hus's death at the hands of foreign prelates, and armed bands of citizens attacked monasteries in the neighbourhood. Czech noblemen sent a protest to the Council of Constance and 452 of them pledged to defend the cause of religious reform. Within a few months a Hussite priest held almost every church in Bohemia.

Open conflict did not come until 1419, when Wenceslas, aghast at the forces he had unwittingly unleashed, demanded the reinstatement of

Carrying a celebratory bouquet of roses, a new graduate of Prague's 600-year-old Charles University pauses with her family to watch the mechanical pageant enacted each hour by the clock on the city's Old Town Hall (see page 115); her young brother holds the cardboard cylinders containing the degree certificates. The graduation ceremony has always been held in the Great Hall of the nearby Carolinum, seat of the university since the 14th Century.

loyalist priests to their parishes. At this news, a Hussite mob stormed the New Town Hall, seized several officials—whom they denounced as "haters of the chalice"—and flung them from the upper-floor windows to their deaths in the market-place below. This first so-called "Defenestration of Prague" was to be re-enacted many times during the city's subsequent turbulent periods. (Probably the most recent instance occurred in 1948, when Jan Masaryk, son of Tomáš Masaryk and Foreign Minister in the Beneš government, was found dead beneath the window of his office in the Černín palace—even though subsequent Communist regimes have always insisted that he was not pushed to his death, but committed suicide.)

Over the fifteen years that followed the first Defenestration, Bohemia became a battleground. On one side were the multinational armies of the papacy, led by Emperor Sigismund (who, after Wenceslas' death in 1419, had become King of Bohemia as well). On the other were the far from cohesive ranks of the Hussites, who had split into moderate and radical factions; the former included many of the merchants and townspeople, whereas the latter were largely peasants who marched aggressively to war from a fortified settlement they had built 60 miles south of Prague and had named after the biblical hill of Tábor.

The Taborites ran their base camp on utopian, almost communistic principles, describing it as "a community of brothers and sisters"; once they set out to do battle—the women marching alongside the men—they became a fearsome army. They had a brilliant commander in Jan Žižka, a country squire who had been dispossessed of his lands and who later became a mercenary. He was a swaggering figure with a black eye-patch, whose thundering effectiveness in combat led the 19th-Century British historian Thomas Carlyle to dub him "Rhinoceros Žižka". His Taborites were mostly peasants bearing peasant arms—pitchforks, scythes and nail-studded flails—but their strength lay in their indomitable spirit, as they marched behind their white flag with its symbolic red chalice and roared out the battle-hymn "O ye warriors of God, who fight in defence of His law" with such fervour that on more than one occasion an opposing force of heavily armed horsemen turned tail and fled without a fight.

Prague had good reason to be grateful to the Taborites when, in July 1420, Sigismund arrived before the city with a gigantic army (numbering, it is said, 100,000 soldiers of 35 different nationalities—including many Czech supporters of the Emperor) that he had brought to Bohemia for the express purpose of exterminating the Czech "heretics". Žižka's fierce defence of the little hill of Vítkov, on the city's eastern outskirts, ensured victory for the 10,000 Hussites, who thereupon knelt down upon the battlefield and sang the *"Te Deum"*. Sigismund again tried to take Prague in November, but his army was once more put to flight.

Thus freed from outside interference, Prague transformed itself into a theocratic city-state, ruled by an assembly of citizens and Hussite priests that began to introduce revolutionary social reforms. By 1431, when the fifth successive imperial crusade had been repulsed by the Czechs, the Pope was ready to sue for peace. Having thus taken the initiative, the papacy used subtle diplomacy to widen the division that had always existed in the Hussite ranks. The moderate reformers—who included the Bohemian nobility—were becoming uneasy at the growing power of the peasant radicals; in Prague, conflicts between the two factions had already led to the destruction of many fine Gothic buildings. In 1434, therefore, the moderates allied themselves with their former enemies, the Czech supporters of the Pope, and defeated the Taborite army at Lipany in eastern Slovakia. The Hussite Wars thus ground to an unsatisfactory end —although, to this day, the Czechs remember them as a supreme example of their people's capacity for courage in the face of heavy odds.

Bohemia now began a rapid decline from its former greatness. Sigismund's death without an heir in 1437 extinguished the line of Charles IV, leaving a power vacuum that was filled by a haphazard succession of monarchs; for this was an age when thrones were commonly passed among the noble families of Europe by treaties of mutual succession and other forms of hard political bargaining. Between 1458 and 1471 George of Poděbrady, a capable Hussite nobleman who became Bohemia's last native-born monarch, ruled as best he could a nation racked by ecclesiastical infighting. But his successors, the Catholic kings of the Jagiełło dynasty from Poland, were usually weak and frequently absent, circumstances that merely exacerbated a further internal struggle: between Bohemia's barons and its burghers over who should play the leading role in the nation's economy. During these years, Prague witnessed yet more violence, including the massacre of monks by Hussites and the Defenestration of an anti-Hussite mayor. By the early 16th Century, Martin Luther had begun his rebellion against the established Church; which meant that the century-old conflict within Bohemia between Hussites and supporters of the papacy now came to be seen within a wider context: the struggle between Protestants and Catholics that was soon to convulse Europe.

The Czech barons and townspeople came together in 1526 to elect as their King, Ferdinand of Habsburg, the future Holy Roman Emperor, in the hope that he would bring domestic concord. Unfortunately, Ferdinand's hostility to Protestantism provoked further unrest in Bohemia that was harshly suppressed—and led to the appearance of Austrian police officers in Czech towns (where they were to remain for almost 400 years). Thereafter, Bohemia was left in relative peace; the Habsburgs were too busy becoming the dominant dynasty in Europe, whilst Catholic Christendom as a whole was more concerned with the threat from the Ottoman Turks, who in 1529 had briefly besieged Vienna, the imperial capital.

By the end of the 16th Century Prague was little more than a provincial backwater—which made it particularly attractive to the Emperor Rudolf II,

A proud mother records her daughters' visit to Czechoslovakia's National Monument on Žižkov Hill, the site of an epic victory won by the Czech military leader Jan Žižka in 1420. Žižka's equestrian statue is backed by the gaunt mausoleum containing the tombs of Communist Presidents and officials and the grave of the Unknown Soldier, a memorial to Czech troops killed in the Second World War.

Ferdinand's grandson, who left Vienna in 1584 and made Prague Castle his imperial palace. Rudolf was a melancholic, secretive man who disliked affairs of state and therefore tried to turn his back upon the enmity between Protestants and Catholics that was crippling the empire—and that would continue to do so until long after his death. He is best remembered as a voracious art collector, who once had a painting by Albrecht Dürer carried gingerly on foot by "four stout men" all the way from Venice to Prague in order to avoid damage in transit.

Rudolf was also obsessed by alchemy, and his court was soon filled with numerous outrageous charlatans in the Emperor's pay. One of them was an Irishman, Edward Kelly, whose ears had been cropped in England for forgery, and who thereupon came to Prague hinting that he could turn a pound of mercury into an ingot of gold by adding to it one drop of a certain red oil. The Emperor did give his patronage to more serious scientists, however, such as the celebrated astronomers Tycho Brahe, a Dane, and Johannes Kepler, a German. Brahe unfortunately fell victim to Rudolf's eccentric rule that guests should not leave his table while he himself still sat there. Having drunk too much one night, the Dane stayed painfully in his place until his bladder ruptured and killed him.

By the time the half-hearted Rudolf had been deposed by his brother Matthias in 1611, the Habsburg dynasty's power was beginning to be challenged by its vassal states throughout Europe. When the imperial succession eventually passed to Ferdinand II, a fanatical Catholic, Bohemia's Protestant nobility—both Czech and German—determined to forestall any attacks on their religion.

The most notorious Defenestration of Prague occurred on May 23, 1618, when the Protestant leaders threw three of Ferdinand's officials down 40 feet from a window in the castle—but a heap of rubbish in the moat broke their fall; they survived to escape from Prague and to tell their imperial master that the Czechs, for all their rebellious noises, were in reality ill equipped, with little prospect of allies. Nevertheless, a year later the Czech assembly defiantly offered the Bohemian crown to Frederick, Elector Palatine, a Calvinist prince from south Germany.

In late 1620 Ferdinand's army of Austrian, Bavarian and Spanish troops invaded Bohemia and marched on Prague. On the evening of November 7 it met the Protestant defenders at the White Mountain, a low hill three miles west of Hradčany. There, the following day, in a sharp two-hour battle, the Czech forces were routed; in places, it is said, their dead lay 12 deep.

The victors exacted a dreadful retribution. To the rolling of drums, 27 Czech leaders were publicly decapitated in the Old Town Square and a dozen of their heads were displayed on the towers of the Charles Bridge. Anyone, whether Protestant or Catholic, who was suspected of harbouring nationalist sentiments had his property confiscated. Nobles and burghers were allowed to emigrate—and it is estimated that 300,000 did so—but

Sunflowers almost reach the eaves of a brightly painted cottage in Golden Lane, a street of minute dwellings inside the walls of Prague Castle. Originally built in the 16th Century as quarters for the castle guards, the cottages later became the abode and work-place of the city's goldsmiths—hence the name of the lane—and also, according to legend, housed the alchemists brought from all over Europe by the eccentric Emperor Rudolf II, who ruled from Prague during the period 1576 to 1611.

the landless peasants were obliged to stay and be forcibly converted to Catholicism. The work of destroying the nation was carried out so thoroughly that the Czechs lost all semblance of political and cultural identity for almost 200 years.

Those centuries were not wholly bleak for the citizens of Prague. The arts, for example, flowered there under Habsburg patronage as gloriously as they had in the days of Charles IV; the city was physically transformed by a wealth of baroque churches and palaces that rivalled in splendour the achievements of the Gothic stonemasons and architects. But such benefits were generally the work of foreigners who had gravitated to Prague from other regions of the Habsburg Empire, filling the vacuum left by the emigration of so many native talents.

By contrast, cultural growth of a specifically Czech kind came to a standstill. The Jesuits, Ferdinand's favourite religious order, exerted a stranglehold over education in Bohemia and harshly censored all literary production; one Jesuit, Antonín Koniáš, boasted of having consigned to the flames more than 60,000 books printed in Czech. The German tongue was given a status equal to that of Czech and eventually became the language of official business in Bohemia. In order to survive, many Czech artists and scholars were obliged to flee the country; of all these emigrants, perhaps the greatest loss to his people was the educational reformer Jan Komenský, generally known as Comenius.

Born into an affluent Moravian family in 1592, Comenius spent his early manhood as a minister of the Moravian Brethren, a Protestant sect. He had already begun to formulate his vision of the regeneration of human society through enlightened education when Habsburg repression forced him to leave the country. From then until his death in 1670 he pursued a distinguished career as a teacher and educational theorist in Poland, Sweden, Prussia, Hungary and Holland. Indeed, if Governor John Winthrop of the new Massachusetts Bay colony in America had had his way, Comenius would have become president of the recently founded Harvard College.

In exile Comenius wrote treatises such as *The Great Didactic*, *The School of Infancy* and *The Gate of Languages Unlocked* that adopted a revolutionary approach to the teaching of the young. "As far as possible," he wrote, "men are to be taught to become wise not by books but by the Heavens, the Earth, the oaks and the beeches; that is, they must learn to know and examine the things themselves and not the observations and testimony of others about things." Comenius argued that education should prepare a child for life, not for formal erudition; it should therefore be conducted in the vernacular rather than in Latin, and punishment should not be handed out for mere intellectual failings. Even today, after many political and cultural vicissitudes, the Czech educational system still owes much to Comenius' ideas.

While Czech *émigrés* were thus enriching the intellectual life of Europe, the humiliation of their homeland continued. In an attempt to efface the memory of Jan Hus, the Catholic rulers fostered a cult associated with his contemporary, John of Nepomuk, a priest whom Wenceslas IV had ordered to be drowned in the Vltava, allegedly for refusing to reveal the secrets of the Queen's confessional—although historians now believe that their dispute concerned Wenceslas' misuse of church property. In 1683 a statue of St. John of Nepomuk was the first to be erected on the Charles Bridge. In the 17th Century Prague's university—another reminder of the Czechs' golden age—was renamed the Charles-Ferdinand University.

By then, the Habsburgs had long since ceased to think of Prague as a mere war trophy. Its economic prosperity—enhanced by large-scale investment in industries such as iron and textiles—had made it one of the most cherished possessions of their empire. Between 1741 and 1757, in the course of the long conflict between Prussia and Austria over hegemony in central Europe, Prague was thrice attacked by the Prussians or their allies; but on each occasion an Austrian army drove them away.

Two hundred years is too long for an imperialist power to maintain a consistently oppressive rule; and few strong national identities can be extinguished for ever. Towards the end of the 18th Century in Bohemia the rulers and the ruled began to reach an accommodation. The enlightened Josef II, Austrian Emperor from 1780 to 1790, largely abolished serfdom on the landed estates of Bohemia and gave the peasantry opportunities for education. By these measures, he hoped to provide contented, well-

A bronze and gilt statue of the Czech martyr, St. John of Nepomuk, stands on the Charles Bridge at the point from which in 1383—according to one tradition—he was thrown into the Vltava to drown, following a dispute with King Wenceslas IV. The effigy—the first of the many baroque statues to be erected on the medieval bridge—was set up when John was canonized in 1683 during the Counter-Reformation; the saint's cult was encouraged by the Jesuits in an attempt to detach the loyalty of the Czechs from their Protestant hero, the 15th-Century reformer, Jan Hus.

trained subjects for his empire; yet, by their stress on political centralization, the reforms unwittingly gave a renewed stimulus to Czech nationalism.

Under Austrian rule, the Czechs had been deprived of their language and, in effect, of their history, and so had lost their sense of national separateness. The first task of the Czech nationalists was therefore to remind their compatriots of Bohemia's past greatness and rich cultural heritage. Patriotic scholars helped to resuscitate the native language by lobbying for its use in Bohemia's schools, and by producing newspapers, novels and poetry in Czech. An equally important contribution was made by historians such as František Palacký, whose *History of the Czech Nation* characterized Bohemia's history as a struggle between Slav and Teuton, and thus provided a clear rationale for the nationalist programme.

The Czechs made a premature bid for independence in 1848, the "Year of Revolutions", when insurrections against Europe's autocratic regimes broke out in Vienna, Paris, Berlin, Milan, Naples, Cracow and Budapest. In Prague, armed students and factory workers—supported by many of the city's bourgeoisie—erected barricades across the narrow streets of the Old Town and demanded the withdrawal from the city of the Austrian garrison. An artillery bombardment subdued the revolt after six days and, thereafter, Habsburg rule tightened in retaliation. Censorship and police activity became harsher and, in 1860, a new constitution for the Czechs confirmed the dominant position of the German inhabitants of Bohemia and Moravia, who by then accounted for about one-third of the population.

The result was growing disillusionment among those conservative Czechs who had hitherto been content with gradual progress towards national self-determination under the protective umbrella of the Austrian Empire. Palacký's change of attitude was typical; by 1865, the man who had once stated that "if the Austro-Hungarian Empire had not existed it would have had to be invented", was defiantly writing: "We were here before Austria and we shall be here after her."

During the last third of the 19th Century outside forces came to the aid of Czech nationalism. In 1866 Otto von Bismarck, the Prussian Prime Minister dedicated to the unification—by the application of "blood and iron"—of all Germans under his own nation's leadership, fought a seven-week war with Franz Josef, the Austrian Emperor, and wiped out his army at Sadová, 60 miles east of Prague. From that point on, the Habsburgs slid into a decline, leaving the way open for a renewal of Czech political ambitions. These were given direct expression by the parties—such as the progressive Young Czechs—that were formed to carry on the business of regional government within the crumbling empire, and whose deputies attended the Imperial Council in Vienna.

But Czech nationalism was demonstrated perhaps most strikingly in the popularity of the Sokol Movement, founded in Prague in 1862 ostensibly to promote gymnastic activity among the young. Throughout the land,

Idealized Slav figures and falcons—symbols of strength—decorate a banknote designed by Mucha in 1919.

Pioneer of Art Nouveau

Ironically, Alphonse Mucha—perhaps the most celebrated modern Czech artist—spent most of his career abroad. Born in 1860 in Moravia, he found few opportunities in his homeland, and made his reputation in Paris, where the art nouveau style he helped to pioneer became known as *le style Mucha*. Nevertheless, Mucha remained a fervent champion of Slav national identity and in 1922, soon after Czechoslovak independence, he returned to devote his talents free of charge to the new state, designing everything from policemen's uniforms to epic murals for public buildings. Sadly, he lived to see the end of his dream; he died in 1939, soon after the Nazis occupied his country.

In a 1912 Mucha poster for a lottery in aid of Czech education, "Slavia" weeps over a child forced under Austrian rule to attend a German-language school.

96/ **A Millennium of Changing Fortunes**

In a 1928 poster, Mucha portrays "Slavia" playing the lyre before an ancestral god whose three faces represent past, present and future.

thousands of Czechs of all ages and social classes joined the organization, which held annual displays in provincial towns and a vast festival (*slet*) in Prague every six years. Alongside pure gymnastics, however, went a busy programme of social activities and frequent uniformed parades conducted with quasi-military discipline. The movement was, in fact, a thinly veiled manifestation of Czech national solidarity; the word *sokol*—meaning literally "falcon"—had long been a synonym for "hero" among Slav peoples.

These years also saw the destinies of the Czechs and Slovaks beginning to converge. Although both were Slavs, their histories had been radically different for a thousand years; the Czechs, in spite of periods of alien domination, had kept pace with the progress of European civilization, whereas the Slovaks, held in continual thrall to Hungarian landowners, had remained an entirely peasant people. Not until the 19th Century did the two discover a common interest in freeing themselves from foreign rule, and the earliest manifestation of a joint political cause was the Slavonic Congress held at Prague in 1848, chiefly to demonstrate to the world the increasing solidarity of the Slav peoples.

The Czechs and the Slovaks were eventually drawn together by a man who had the blood of both nations running in his veins: Tomáš Garrigue Masaryk, the son of a Slovak coachman and a Moravian housemaid. After studying in Vienna and later in Leipzig—where he met his future wife, an American music student—Masaryk was in 1882 appointed Professor of Philosophy at Prague's Charles-Ferdinand University. He began to share in the capital's political life and soon made a name for himself as a moderate nationalist who opposed the romantic, uncritical patriotism then current among many Czechs. In 1886, for example, he proved that the Czech epic poems in the supposedly medieval Králův Dvůr and Zelena Hora manuscripts—which some nationalists held up as evidence that Czech literature had a longer and more distinguished history than it was usually credited with—were in fact forgeries by the Czech poet who "discovered" them in 1817. In order to counter the equally impractical radicalism of the Czech nationalist Left, Masaryk eventually founded his own political party, the Realists, largely composed of moderate intellectuals.

Up to 1914, Masaryk worked quietly for an improvement in Czech political autonomy within the framework of Austrian rule, inspired by his belief that small central European nations needed some kind of protection against the greater threat of Germany. But the outbreak of the First World War—during which Austria was allied with Germany against the Western Allies and Russia—changed his mind. He promptly exiled himself to Paris and there, together with Edvard Beneš, a Czech sociology lecturer, and Milan Štefánik, a Slovak astronomer serving in the French Army, formed the Czech Committee Abroad. Its purpose was to enlist the sympathies of other exiles then living in France, Britain, Russia and the U.S.A. for an unconditional Czechoslovak independence. As the war progressed, Czech

In an allegorical portrait painted in 1934 by the Austrian artist, Oscar Kokoschka, the aging Tomáš Masaryk, first President of the Czechoslovak Republic, is shown seated in front of a vista of central Prague. On the left looms the shadowy figure of the 17th-Century educational reformer Comenius, symbolizing the Czech nation's long Humanistic tradition.

and Slovak conscripts in the Austrian armies that were fighting the Russians on the Eastern Front began to go over to the enemy in their thousands. In 1917 Masaryk went to Russia, where Kerensky's provisional post-Tsarist government allowed him to organize these prisoners of war into an independent Czechoslovak Legion that would fight for the Allied cause in the east. By November, however, Kerensky had been toppled by the Bolsheviks and, in March 1918, the new regime made peace with Germany—a development that caused Masaryk to leave Russia. The Western Allies now wished to use the Czechoslovak Legion—their only reliable confederates left inside Russia—to fight the Red Army. But the Czech Committee in Paris opted for non-involvement in Russia's affairs and ordered the 42,000 legionaries stranded there to escape eastwards across Asia.

The Czechoslovak Legion commandeered locomotives and rolling stock of the Trans-Siberian Railway and steamed the 5,000 miles to Vladivostok, fighting off repeated attacks by the Bolshevik forces. Once arrived, the legionaries boarded Allied ships bound for Europe—although some stragglers did not reach Prague until the mid-1920s. The legion's exploits, widely reported in the world's Press, were largely responsible for bringing the cause of Czechoslovak independence to the notice of the West.

But Masaryk's international diplomacy had played an equally important part. After leaving Russia, he had sailed to the U.S.A. to talk to President

Woodrow Wilson. In Wilson's recently issued peace proposals, the famous "Fourteen Points", he had strongly advocated "self-determination for all nations"; so the Czech leader was eventually able to enlist Wilson's support for the liberation from the Austrian yoke of all Slav people. Masaryk also employed his powers of persuasion on a U.S. domestic lobby; at that time there were said to be more Czechs living in Chicago than in any city other than Prague.

In September 1918 the United States followed France and Britain in recognizing Masaryk's committee in Paris as the provisional government of a new Republic of Czechoslovakia. On October 18, Masaryk and Beneš made a simultaneous declaration of Czechoslovak independence. A month later, the First World War came to an end.

During the last few days of Habsburg rule, there were demonstrations in the streets of Prague; but they were little different in kind from the demonstrations then going on in other European cities to mark Armistice Day. The double-headed eagle, symbol of the Habsburgs, was removed from Prague's government buildings, causing some damage to masonry. A crowd demolished the baroque statue of the Virgin Mary in the Old Town Square, thus clearing the spot where in 1621 the Czech Protestant leaders had been beheaded after the Battle of the White Mountain, and leaving the square to be dominated by the enormous memorial to Jan Hus which the Austrians had allowed to be unveiled only three years earlier. Otherwise, the Czechs entered into independence peacefully and their former Austrian masters simply acquiesced.

On November 14, 1918, Tomáš Masaryk, architect of that independence, was elected first President of the Czechoslovak Republic at the inaugural meeting of the National Assembly—the first representative, democratic parliament that the Slav peoples of Bohemia, Moravia and Slovakia had ever had. By now 68 years old, Masaryk set out upon this great new venture with an idealism untainted by his years of political struggle. He shared with Comenius and the Hussites the vision of a humane, enlightened society, and would henceforth attempt to bring it to reality; "Tábor," he said, "is our programme."

From the start, the new republic enjoyed several distinct advantages. It was democratic in complexion; under Austrian rule, there had been no indigenous Czech ruling class, and so a new élite now had to be recruited from among the bourgeoisie and the workers. Fortunately, the existing civil service—largely Czech in composition—was efficient and incorrupt. Czechoslovakia also had considerable economic potential. Its 13.6 million inhabitants represented one-quarter of the former Austro-Hungarian Empire's population and occupied one-fifth of its area—the remainder having been shared out among the new republics of Poland and Yugoslavia, the kingdom of Romania, and a shrunken Austria and Hungary. Yet, the Czechs inherited two-thirds of the old empire's industry—although

Parading before thousands of Praguers in 1920, members of the Sokol gymnastic league carry the head of an enormous statue of Liberty erected to mark the first of the movement's six-yearly festivals to take place after the establishment of the Republic of Czechoslovakia in 1918. Founded in 1862 and dedicated to physical and moral betterment, Sokol (meaning "Falcon") became one of the rallying-points of the Czech nationalist movement in the 19th and early 20th Centuries. The league was later suppressed during the Nazi occupation, and was finally abolished by the Communists in 1948.

this was concentrated in Bohemia and Moravia rather than in the predominantly agricultural region of Slovakia.

The name of Škoda, hitherto associated with the manufacture of armaments for the Austrian Empire, now began to appear on the front of Czech motor cars. Tomáš Bat'a, who had supplied boots to the Imperial Army, became, after Czechoslovakia's independence, the world's largest manufacturer of civilian footwear. This he achieved by building a huge, highly mechanized factory—consciously modelled on contemporary U.S. practice—at Zlín in eastern Moravia, and by offering his employees a wide range of cash incentives and fringe benefits in return for their unconditional loyalty to the firm. Other large enterprises in Czechoslovakia manufactured electrical generators, glassware, textiles and machine-guns, most of which were exported. But the most distinctive feature of Czech economic policy was its encouragement of small businesses; by 1930, 91 per cent of all the nation's concerns employed five workers or less. This was entirely in keeping with Masaryk's humane approach to government. He led a small, vulnerable nation—and he firmly believed to the end of his days in cherishing the small things and making them good.

Czechoslovakia was born with problems too, some of which were never satisfactorily solved. There was the question of the minorities: the four million Slovaks and three million Germans who were citizens of a state dominated by six and a half million Czechs. Compared with Bohemia and Moravia, Slovakia was a backward area, reckoned to be 70 years behind its neighbours in economic terms. The appointment of Czechs to important posts in Slovakia, essential to the recovery of the region, provoked much resentment among a people who yielded to no one in their pride. But there was often no alternative; when the first Slovak university was founded at Bratislava, the regional capital, in 1919, only 10 adequately trained Slovak candidates were forthcoming for the senior teaching posts. Czechoslovakia's German inhabitants were disaffected from the start, despite the fact that Germans served in successive national governments.

The new nation was also hampered by disagreements between the members of those governments, which were always coalitions—an inevitable circumstance in a country that had arrived at independence with a large number of political parties whose views ranged from far Left to far Right. Yet, in spite of some friction (usually alleviated by Masaryk's benign intervention) a surprising amount of enlightened legislation was enacted. Indeed, Czechoslovakia's domestic policies—particularly in areas such as public housing, land reform, education and social services—were among the most progressive in the world at that period.

In all this, the guiding hand of Masaryk could be seen. As President, he was supposed to be above politics—the father figure watching over the nation from his suite of rooms in Prague Castle. In practice, he was often to be found gently bullying government ministers into accepting his farsighted plans. He surrounded himself with a set known as the Castle Group that included few politicians but, instead, the senior civil servants who carried out the actual business of government, and the academics and writers whose ideas could influence the nation as a whole. Every Friday night the group met at the house of Karel Čapek, the playwright, in order to receive fresh directives from the "Old Gentleman". At other times its members were busy whispering in this ear or that ear, moulding government policy behind the scenes—much to the annoyance of politicians of the extreme Right and Left, who resented the Castle Group's unofficial power and moderate views.

But Masaryk's position was impregnable. He had transformed a subject people into a sane, democratic nation; as a result, distinguished early fugitives from Nazism such as Thomas Mann sought shelter in Prague. Masaryk was secure in the affections of the Czech people not primarily because he was a thinker but because he had been born poor and had made good, and because his outstanding virtues were courage, compassion and common sense. In the Czech pantheon his only rival was Charles IV, who had also built a proud nation from a wasted people.

In 1935 the "Old Gentleman"—by now a tired, sick man of 85—abdicated the presidency, and two years later he died. The Czechs grieved as they had rarely grieved before; for, in the words of their neighbour, Adolf Hitler, they already sensed the doom of their nation.

4

Preserving the Magnificent Past

Prague is, quite simply, one of the most beautiful cities in the world, and the especial marvel is that the beauty is almost entirely man-made. Had man never settled here, you would have encountered a pleasant, meandering river with a ridge of high ground overlooking one bank and a gentle slope undulating away from the other—attractive enough, but no more so than thousands of other spots in Europe. Yet, 30 generations of builders in stone have given Prague the majesty and the lyricism that can take your breath away, and nature has simply provided the grace notes—such as the luxuriant gardens that spill down the slope below the castle on the ridge of Hradčany, or the 30,000 trees that today line the streets, squares and parks of the city.

Prague's survival into the late 20th Century as a medieval, Renaissance and baroque city, substantially unaltered since the 18th Century, has largely been a matter of luck. Enemies have often besieged it, but seldom sacked it; neither Hitler's Luftwaffe nor the Allied air forces bombed it; and, throughout the centuries, its population growth has been remarkably slow. The city's ancient centre has been allowed to remain what it was. Successive generations of Praguers have been content to use the buildings erected by their forefathers; and, although factories and high-rise apartment blocks are gradually multiplying on the outskirts, old Prague remains to this day a living, and lived-in, entity that is far more than a mere museum of magnificent architecture

Of all Prague's visual delights, the grandest is the ridge of Hradčany. While the guidebooks insist that Prague, like Rome, is built on seven hills, most of these "hills" seem to me little more than humps in the ground. Although not the highest, Hradčany approaches epic scale as it towers 850 feet above the city. Its summit overlooking the west bank of the Vltava is crowned by the massive walls of Prague Castle, with the three ornate spires of St. Vitus' Cathedral shooting up from within them.

The castle was founded in the 9th Century as a rude hilltop stronghold enclosed by a wooden stockade and, 300 years later, was rebuilt in stone as a perfect medieval fortress defended by battlements, towers and a moat. But time, assisted by a great fire in 1541, has wrought many changes. The Prague Castle you see today, a wedge-shaped complex about 500 yards long by 150 yards wide, looks more like a palace than a fortress, for its cliff-like outer walls are largely 18th Century in origin and are studded with rows of windows that glitter in the sun. Grouped around the three courtyards within those walls, however, are buildings that have

A pair of robust nudes sculpted in the florid manner of the 1890s frame the doorway of a private house in Prague's Josefov district. During the last epoch of the Austro-Hungarian Empire, the decorative art nouveau style reflected in these statues found a sympathetic following in Prague, where its proponents inherited a tradition of elaborate ornamentation begun 200 years earlier during the baroque era.

Seen from the city centre, the buildings along the crest of the great natural ridge of Hradčany present a floodlit panorama of Prague's architectural heritage. Most prominent is St. Vitus' Cathedral (centre), whose sombre mass—begun in the 14th Century, but not completed until the 19th—soars behind the many-windowed 18th-Century façade of Prague Castle. At the far right rise the twin Romanesque towers of St. George's, consecrated in A.D. 925.

survived from every period of the castle's history, and a surprisingly large proportion of them are still in regular use.

The ordinary visitor enters Prague Castle through an impressive architectural sequence at its westernmost extremity: first, through a wrought-iron gate flanked by pairs of stone giants writhing in combat; then across the elegant First Courtyard, built by Viennese architects in the 1760s, to the sober Matthias Gate of 1614; and thence into the Second Courtyard, one of the busiest parts of the castle complex.

The range of 17th-Century buildings that forms the south side of the Second Courtyard now contains the official reception rooms of the President of Czechoslovakia; black, fish-shaped Tatras—the most luxurious product of the Czech automobile industry—regularly sweep through the Matthias Gate to draw up outside on official business. On the north side of the quadrangle is the florid 16th-Century Spanish Hall, dating from the time of Rudolf II and restored in the 19th Century. The Central Committee of the Czech Communist Party is likely to be holding some weighty meeting here—which is why those two young soldiers stand so sternly to attention outside the entrance, to be relieved at intervals by another pair who march across the courtyard with the same kind of goose-step that is used by the guards on duty outside Lenin's mausoleum in Moscow's Red Square.

But anyone is free to wander on through the gate in the east wall—as thousands do on fine summer days—in order to visit the extraordinary variety of buildings that lie in the Third Courtyard beyond. Visitors may tour the old Royal Palace on the south side of the courtyard, and inspect the spacious rooms of the Imperial Court Chancellery, where the 27 Czech leaders of the anti-Habsburg revolt were sentenced to death after the Battle of the White Mountain in 1620, or the old imperial stables, which now house part of the collections of Czechoslovakia's National Gallery—including masterpieces by Titian, Tintoretto and Rubens.

Most magnificent of these royal apartments is the Vladislav Hall, built for Vladislav Jagiełło, the Polish-born King who ruled Bohemia between 1471 and 1516. Beneath its vaulted roof, whose curved and interlaced stone ribs are reminiscent of the boughs of trees, the nobility of Bohemia for three centuries gathered to pay homage to their newly crowned monarchs. These coronation ceremonies also included a jousting tournament—and you can still inspect the broad, shallow Riders' Staircase up which horsemen spurred their steeds to gain access to the competition taking place within the hall itself. Since 1935, six successive Presidents of the Republic have been elected in the Vladislav Hall at special sessions of the Czech National Assembly.

Diagonally across from the Royal Palace, on the courtyard's eastern side, stands the Basilica of St. George, one of Prague's most venerable ecclesiastical monuments; its twin 12th-Century towers and Renaissance

façade conceal a structure that dates largely from the 10th Century. And beyond the Third Courtyard, at the easternmost end of the castle, are the 16 little cottages of Golden Lane, where, according to a popular but unsubstantiated tradition, Rudolf II's alchemists are said to have lived; the cottages are now occupied by souvenir-sellers who enjoy a thriving trade purveying stamps and guidebooks to the tourists.

But none of the buildings on Hradčany can compete in grandeur with the Cathedral of St. Vitus, which stands in the centre of the Third Courtyard. Its Gothic southern tower, capped by a curious baroque spire, rises from the heart of the castle to a height of 300 feet, and the twin western steeples, erected in the 19th Century, are only slightly less lofty; together they create the unforgettable skyline that, wherever you may be in Prague, draws the eye like a magnet. Inside the cathedral is vast space—the nave, for example, is 118 feet high—embellished by the artefacts of several centuries; for although St. Vitus' was begun by Charles IV in the 1340s, the vicissitudes of Prague's history delayed the final completion of its western end until 1929.

Perhaps the most appealing of the treasures in the cathedral are those set in the wall of the gallery high above each nave arcade. There, looking benignly down on the congregation, are 21 portrait busts of the cathedral's earliest benefactors—including Charles and his family—that were carved 600 years ago in the stonemason's workshop of Peter Parler, a German architect who worked on the building. Elsewhere in St. Vitus' there are 19 chapels crammed with splendid furnishings from all ages, including some of the most dazzling examples anywhere of 20th-Century stained glass.

St. Vitus' is indisputably the greatest memorial to the Christian monarchs who once ruled from Prague. It contains the tombs of seven kings of Bohemia, among them Charles himself, George of Poděbrady, and the Habsburg Emperor Rudolf II, and those of earlier Přemyslid rulers. The crown jewels of Bohemia—which include the magnificent, gem-encrusted crown of St. Wenceslas, remodelled for Charles IV from an 11th-Century heirloom—are kept in the crypt behind seven locks, each of whose keys is held, according to an ancient custom, in the custody of a different institution of this Communist state. No visitor can see the treasures of St. Vitus' without beginning to feel Prague's history seeping into his bones.

And no visitor should descend from the heights of Hradčany without first making his way westward along the ridge to the monastery of Strahov. One good reason is to enjoy what is to my mind the most splendid of all views of Prague: straight down the Vltava to the south, with the rooftops and innumerable towers of the city spreading away on either bank of the river. The other reason is the monastery itself, founded in 1140 for the Premonstratensian order of canons but largely rebuilt in the late 17th Century. By then, baroque art and architecture were reaching their flourishing height; the soaring, angular lines of the Gothic—an appeal to

Dwarfed by two vigorous groups of sculpted giants surmounting the massive gateposts, white-gloved sentries guard the main entrance to Prague Castle's outer courtyard. Built on the site of the city's earliest fortress, the castle once housed the kings of Bohemia, and nowadays accommodates the President of the Republic and the headquarters of the Communist Party.

the spiritual side of man's nature—had long since given way to a new style whose generous curves spoke more directly to the emotions.

You will not see monks at Strahov these days for in 1953 the monastery became the national museum of Czech literature, housing 130,000 rare books and manuscripts in the native tongue, and a reconstruction of a 16th-Century printing shop. Strahov—or, as it is now called, the Memorial of National Literature—is only one of nearly 40 museums and art galleries in Prague, but it is undoubtedly the most splendid.

The former monastery is one of Prague's finest baroque buildings; behind its deceptively plain exterior there are rooms and galleries where white, stuccoed walls rise to painted ceilings on which swirling saints, prophets and putti posture against a vivid blue sky. Most marvellous of them all is the Theological Hall, a long, rather low gallery with a tunnel-vaulted roof and walls completely lined with bookcases full of theological works bound in dark leather or ancient white hide. Above the topmost shelves the ceiling arches upward into a confection of white plasterwork surrounding painted panels by Father Siard Nosecký, an 18th-Century canon, showing allegorical figures and scenes from the Book of Proverbs. It is a vision that makes you reluctant to return to the world outside.

The finest way to descend from the heights of Hradčany is to stroll down the broad flight of steps that hugs the southern wall of the castle complex. As you go down, the panorama of Prague gradually disappears behind the pink, pantiled roofs and gabled housefronts of Malá Strana, with a few church spires and the great baroque dome of St. Nicholas' Church poking up above them. Walking through this historic district in the shadow of the castle, you will eventually arrive in little Malá Strana Square, from which narrow, cobbled streets wind away in all directions; tramcars clatter through some of them, almost brushing the houses on each side.

Down here, you can at last begin to enjoy the distinctive flavour of old Prague, which mixes the homely and the splendid to a remarkable degree. Each morning, you will see housewives sweeping their doorsteps and, at dusk, an old-fashioned lamplighter comes round with his long pole to ignite the gas street-lamps. Yet, within a few yards of such domestic scenes you are quite likely to come across a magnificent palace.

For Prague is a city of palaces: there are 55 of them, mostly built between the 17th and 19th Centuries for the great noble families of Bohemia, but nowadays used as embassies, government offices and museums. Many of these dynasties, such as the Černins and the Vrtbas, were of Czech origin, but some others, such as the Bucquoys and the Liechtensteins, were founded by foreign generals who had fought for the Habsburgs in 1620 and been rewarded with confiscated Czech estates.

The street called Letenská will serve to illustrate the district's characteristic mixture. After wriggling out of Malá Strana Square, it settles

Shelves crammed with religious books and manuscripts line the walls of the Theological Hall, a richly decorated baroque library in Strahov, formerly a monastery and now the home of the national collection of literature in the Czech language. The paintings on the ceiling—lively allegories illustrating the Book of Proverbs—are by Father Siard Nosecký, an 18th-Century resident of Strahov who spent more than 20 years embellishing the building.

down into a long curve, the right-hand side of which is occupied by a continuous row of private houses. On the left, at the beginning of the curve, is the tavern called U sv. Tomáše (At St. Thomas'), founded in 1358, and where, at almost any time of the day or night, you will find working people consuming large quantities of beer and food in a dark, barrel-vaulted cellar. Beyond that, the left-hand side of Letenská consists of a long, blank, stone wall with a little wooden door at the far end. Open that door and you will step right into the garden of the Waldstein (Wallenstein) Palace, which is very grand indeed.

The palace was built for one of the most colourful opportunists in Czech history, born Albrecht Václav z Valdštejn in a small Bohemian town in 1583. Of aristocratic blood, he was a professional soldier in the service of the Czech Estates—Protestant lords and knights of Bohemia and Moravia who, even after the Catholic Habsburgs had come to rule Bohemia in the 16th Century, remained powerful enough to preserve certain ancient constitutional rights. In 1606, however, in order to ingratiate himself with the ruling Habsburgs, Valdštejn turned Catholic. Three years later, his Jesuit confessor arranged for him to marry an elderly Catholic widow who owned immense estates in Moravia.

During the revolt of 1618, when Bohemia's Protestant nobility rose against the Emperor Ferdinand II, the rebels confiscated these lands from Waldstein (who had by then Germanized the spelling of his name). In retaliation for this seizure, Waldstein brought to Ferdinand's support a cavalry regiment commanded by himself and did much to help the Habsburgs win at the White Mountain. His reward was the governorship of Bohemia and a partnership in a mint, the proceeds of which enabled him to buy up 60 estates that had belonged to the defeated Czechs.

Such was Waldstein's wealth that he planned his palace in Prague to rival that city's castle in size and splendour. From 1623 onwards, craftsmen were brought from Italy to design and embellish a building that, together with its grounds, swallowed up an area formerly occupied by 28 houses and gardens. On the ceiling of its Great Hall a grandiose fresco depicts Waldstein himself as Mars, god of war, riding triumphantly in his chariot.

In 1625 Ferdinand appointed Waldstein generalissimo of the imperial armies, which were by now embroiled in the Thirty Years' War—a complex struggle, involving many nations in a conflict between the Habsburg Holy Roman Emperor and the German princes and cities for control of central Europe. On behalf of the Habsburgs, Waldstein won some spectacular victories over the Hungarians, the Danes and the Protestant princes of Germany. But success went to the great general's head. He decided to take an independent line and began secret negotiations with the Emperor's enemies. His ambitions were said to include the crown of Bohemia, his own kingdom in Germany and even a crusade to recover Constantinople from the Turks. Waldstein was becoming a distinct threat

110/ **Preserving the Magnificent Past**

On Petřín Hill—at 1,060 feet the highest point in central Prague—wooded parkland encircles 18th-Century St. Lawrence's Church and its chapel.

to the Emperor; so in 1634, at the west Bohemian fortress of Cheb, he was stabbed to death by an Irish mercenary in the pay of the Habsburgs.

Nowadays, Waldstein's palace is mostly used as government offices, although ordinary Praguers are free to wander through its formal gardens. There, a grid pattern of neatly clipped hedges encloses innumerable flower beds. Fountains splash into shell-shaped stone basins stocked with large goldfish. On an islet in the small lake two swans have made their nest. The *salá terrena* or Garden Hall—a colossal, colonnaded summerhouse—looks down an avenue lined with 17th-Century classical bronze effigies. Among them is the most delightfully vulgar fountain in Prague: a mother-and-child group that emits three thin jets of water—two from the woman's nipples and one from the infant's crotch.

Malá Strana is full of such small delights. One could spend half a day, for example, searching out the old painted or carved house-signs that still survive there in considerable numbers. In a single street that runs parallel with the Castle Steps, you can find houses known as At the Golden Wheel, At the White Angel, At the Red Eagle and At the Two Suns.

Eastward from Malá Strana, across the Charles Bridge, lie Prague's Old Town (Staré Město) founded in the 10th Century, and the surrounding New Town (Nové Město), dating from the 14th Century. Both districts have always represented workaday Prague, the city of bustling marketplaces, as opposed to the more formal treasures on the other side of the Vltava. But this is not to say that they are visually any less splendid or fascinating than their neighbours on the west bank.

Following the destruction of many of their original buildings during the Hussite Wars, both the Old and the New Towns were elaborately rebuilt in baroque style under the Habsburgs. Among the best individual buildings from that period are several churches—such as St. Nicholas' in the Old Town and the New Town's St. John on the Rock and St. Katherine's—that were designed between 1720 and 1751 by Kilian Ignaz Dientzenhofer, a brilliant and prolific Prague-born architect who was responsible for more than 60 works throughout Bohemia, including 10 churches in Prague alone. These are usually tucked away down twisting, ancient streets, so that their handsome and lavishly frescoed interiors, flooded with light from the numerous windows, come as an unexpected and pleasant surprise to the casual wanderer.

Apart from Dientzenhofer's masterpieces, there are today about 80 other churches and chapels in Prague. In 1949 the Gottwald regime nationalized them all, together with church property throughout Czechoslovakia, and, since then, the State has been responsible for the upkeep of religious buildings and has paid the wages of the clergy.

The price demanded in return has been obedience. At his ordination, every priest, of whatever domination, is required by law to swear an oath

Signs that Talk

The house-signs that adorn many of Prague's old doorways were made for a practical purpose, but like so much else in the city they have their own charm, born of the Praguers' genius for ornamental design.

From the 14th Century until 1770, when street numbering was introduced by the Austro-Hungarian bureaucracy, hanging signboards or sculpted emblems of wood, stone, metal or plaster were the principal means of identifying individual homes. The names of the easily recognized and remembered objects they depicted were adopted as house-names with the addition of the prefix "u"—meaning "at": for example, *U Zlatého Klíče*—At the Golden Key (bottom row, right). Such was the appeal of the signs that the practice, even when no longer necessary, continued well into the 19th Century.

Some motifs were chosen to indicate the trade or profession of the householder—such as the elegant fiddles (top row, second from left) adopted by a family of violin-makers. But most were random choices, inspired by the whim of the owner or of the artist he employed.

In the century or so since the old house-names dropped out of use, many signs have been neglected. As examples, see At the Green Crayfish (top row, second from right) and At the Red Lion (bottom row, second from left) which have long since lost all their distinctive colouring. But the fresh paintwork on other signs, such as At the Three Feathers (middle row, right), is a cheering reminder that present-day Praguers still take pride in the abundance of charming details that embellish their city.

114/ **Preserving the Magnificent Past**

Flanked by statuary, the Old Town Hall clock's dials record the ascendant zodiacal sign, the motions of the sun and moon and the date and time.

As the clock strikes the hour the two small windows set above the main dial (exterior view, opposite) open automatically. Behind each window, six life-size wooden statues of the Apostles rotate on spokes attached to an axle. The two axles are co-ordinated by a binding chain, creating the illusion that a constant procession of 12 saints is passing from one window to the other. The figures have been replaced several times in the clock's 500-year history; the present models substitute for those destroyed when retreating Nazi troops blew up part of the Old Town Hall in 1945.

of loyalty to the secular government. Officially, Czechoslovakia's citizens have complete freedom to follow whatever faith they choose; but the authorities have long taken active measures against organized religion, such as the closing down of theological colleges and the dissemination of atheistic propaganda in schools.

In view of the government's hostile attitude, no official figures exist for the number of practising Christians in Czechoslovakia; but they are unlikely to exceed about 30 per cent of the population and, in the majority of cases, the congregations are mostly made up of old people. Yet the churches themselves are cared for as national treasures of architecture.

Beyond the eastern gate-tower of the Charles Bridge is the narrow entrance to Karlova, one of the main thoroughfares of the Old Town. Here again you can find the special Prague blend of the domestic and the magnificent: on one side of the street there are unpretentious shops, on the other the Clementinum, a colossal 17th-Century building that occupies more ground than any other structure in Prague save the castle. Once a Jesuit seminary, and later the seat of the Charles-Ferdinand University, it now houses the state library. The charm of Karlova, apart from its architecture, lies in the fact that its course is practically unaltered since medieval days, so that it is narrow, wayward and full of sharp bends. It is essentially a street that was created by people who travelled about on foot or on horseback, rather than in wheeled vehicles.

Karlova's destination is the Malé náměstí, or Small Square, where narrowness at last gives way to space. There is room for a fountain enclosed within a flamboyant cage of 16th-Century wrought iron; room, too, for the pedestrian to stand back and admire the eccentric rooftops that

In compliance with national custom, the ornate façade of a 19th-Century synagogue in the New Town is decorated for May Day with Czechoslovak and Soviet flags. Prague has seven synagogues; but the thriving Jewish community they once served was decimated by the Nazis so that, today, only two of the buildings are still used as places of worship; the remainder are museums of Jewish art and life.

surround the square, no two of which are quite alike. Of the houses themselves, At the White Lion catches the eye with its original Gothic doorway; there, in 1488, the first Bible to be printed in Prague was made.

A few minutes' stroll from this quiet spot will bring you to the Staroměstské náměstí, or Old Town Square, where some of the most stirring events in the city's history have occurred. In the Prague Municipal Museum there is a famous exhibit that occupies almost an entire room: an accurate cardboard scale-model of Prague made in 1830. If you compare the miniature Old Town Square there with the real thing, you can see what has changed in a century and a half. The 17th-Century column glorifying the Virgin Mary has given way to the 20th-Century statue honouring Jan Hus. Half of the Old Town Hall is missing because Hitler's troops blew it up the day before they surrendered in May 1945, destroying two neo-Gothic wings and many of the city's ancient archives; the Czechs have left the gap unrepaired as a lasting reproach to an act of wanton vandalism in a city whose other buildings survived the war intact.

Apart from this reminder, the Old Town Square remains as it was, the product of a gradual growth from the Middle Ages to the 19th Century, dignified by two of Prague's finest churches: the Gothic Church of St. Mary of Týn and Dientzenhofer's baroque St. Nicholas'. The houses round the square are mostly Renaissance or baroque in style, although many of them stand upon Romanesque or Gothic foundations. Not one of these buildings is particularly grand—at least not in the manner of, say, the palaces of Malá Strana—but every one of them is handsome and substantial, a monument to European civilization at its most reassuring.

The Old Town Square is much used by Praguers—and not only when they gather together en masse to demonstrate their deepest feelings, as they did, for example, in the passionate days of 1968. They are forever walking across it to reach other parts of the Old Town; they patronize the wine shop called U Bindrů (At Binder's), with its Romanesque vault; and on Saturdays they arrive in their dozens to get married—for the Old Town Hall is the most popular place for civil wedding ceremonies.

On summer days, scores of people idle on the benches surrounding the Hus memorial, watching the goings-on or simply soaking up the sunshine. Life does not leave the Old Town Square until well into the hours of darkness, when the municipal water cart comes rumbling along to spray the cobblestones clean, ready for another day.

The most famous single attraction in the square is without doubt the Orloj, the ancient clock that adorns the tower of the Old Town Hall. Originally constructed in 1410, it is an ingenious combination of art and technology. In the middle is the clock itself, with a complex dial that indicates not only the time of day but also the movements of the sun, moon and planets. Below the dial is the calendarium, a circle of paintings depicting the Signs of the Zodiac and the Labours of the Months. But it is

Tombstones crowd the Jewish cemetery in the Old Town, where some 12,000 persons were interred between 1493 and 1787, when the graveyard was closed. Since Prague's Jews were forbidden to bury their dead elsewhere in the city, coffins had been superimposed on one another, sometimes as many as 12 deep.

the device at the top of the Orloj that, just before the hour strikes, causes passers-by to linger in an expectant group in the square below.

On the hour, two small doors spring open revealing figures of the Twelve Apostles that troop in procession from one side to the other. Meanwhile, alongside the clock-face a skeleton symbolizing Death pulls a bell-rope with one hand and brandishes an hourglass in the other. When the last Apostle has disappeared, a cockerel in a niche above the doorways flaps his wings and crows. Finally, the bell of the Old Town Hall strikes the hour. And generally you will also hear a small volley of applause from the spectators down below.

Most of these spectators are probably on vacation. Each year, an estimated 1.5 million foreign tourists visit this city, about two-thirds of them from other Warsaw Pact countries. Although there is a steady flow of German tourists, Westerners do not come to Prague in anything like the numbers in which they visit the other historic cities of central Europe, such as Vienna or Munich. There are no doubt many reasons for their absence: ignorance of the attractions of the Czech capital; reluctance to risk the discomforts of reputed over-pricing and poor service in hotels that do not come up to Western standards; and perhaps a certain nervousness about visiting a country within the Soviet bloc.

If you stroll out of the Old Town Square in almost any direction, you will be back in a maze of medieval thoroughfares much like Karlova. You will pass through Prague's ancient core along narrow, cobbled alleys or along streets where the buildings on both sides are built out on arcades over the pavement, giving a sensation akin to walking around a monastic

118/ **Preserving the Magnificent Past**

Tracking through a light dusting of winter snow, Praguers in twos and threes cross the Old Town Square, heart of the old city since the 11th Century.

cloister. Yet, even in the narrowest places, surprises are always likely to occur. A great gateway appears in a wall, disclosing a courtyard surrounded at several levels by balconies from which washing hangs to dry, while housewives gossip with their neighbours amid rows of carefully tended pot plants. The Old Town's buildings are by no means the only aspects of its past to have survived; many age-old patterns of urban life still thrive there too. The Praguers buy their food at street markets or in dark little shops, surroundings in which a supermarket would seem a gross violation of scale. People dwell in those streets as their forebears have done for centuries, as comfortably as in an old slipper.

Three hundred yards north-west of the Old Town Square you will find yourself in the district of Josefov, where Prague's thriving Jewish quarter was located until the Second World War. Its ancient cemetery and six fully appointed synagogues are an astonishing discovery to make in a city that was occupied by the Nazis for six years; and the reason for the survival is, indeed, grotesque. When Hitler's troops arrived in Prague, they carefully and methodically preserved all the articles they found in Josefov; for when the Nazis' New Order had at last been established throughout Europe, Prague was to be the place where good Aryans could come to study the material culture of the race that their fathers had wiped off the face of the earth.

There had been a Jewish community in Prague for at least a thousand years. Excluded from full participation in the town's life for centuries, the Jews lived in a cramped, enclosed ghetto in Josefov—until in 1848 they finally received full civil and political rights. The ghetto's alley-ways were eventually demolished and redeveloped; yet anti-Semitism lingered in the 19th Century among the Czechs, largely because many local Jews were of German origin and therefore shared with the other German inhabitants of Bohemia a hostility to Czech nationalism. The Jewish community never recovered from the results of the Nazi period; today there are scarcely more than a thousand Praguers who affirm their Jewish origins.

Josefov's Jewish Town Hall is a 16th-Century building reconstructed in 1763; its picturesque, bulbous clock-tower has a dial marked with Hebrew letters and hands that, to a Gentile, seem to go backwards as they follow the anti-clockwise arrangement of the numerals. Nearby is the great gable of the so-called "Old-New" Synagogue, built in about 1270 and therefore probably the oldest surviving synagogue in Europe; from its vault hangs the banner presented to Prague's Jews by the Emperor Ferdinand III for their help in defending the city in 1648 during the Thirty Years' War. Four other synagogues in Josefov have become museums of Jewish life and art, stocked with the items gathered by the Nazis during the occupation. There are especially fine collections of silver ritual objects, and textiles such as temple curtains. The Pinkas Synagogue, founded in 1479, is now a memorial to the murdered Jews of Bohemia and Moravia; its inside walls are engraved with the names of every one of the 77,297 known concentration camp victims and the date of their deportation.

But the most evocative place in Josefov is the Old Cemetery, with its 12,000 ancient gravestones bearing Hebrew epitaphs. Today, the most frequently visited grave is that of Rabbi Löw—Yehuda Löw ben Bezalel— who died in 1609. During his lifetime the Rabbi was famed throughout Europe as a teacher and scholar, but in later centuries his reputation came to rest on a less plausible achievement: the supposed creation of the Golem, a giant figure made of clay but brought to life, according to Hebrew folklore, by the insertion of cabbalistic formulae in its mouth. The Golem is said to have performed various tasks at the Rabbi's bidding, and it has something of the delicious horror of Frankenstein's monster. The myth is still powerful enough to attract a steady trickle of visitors to this obscure corner of Prague. No one has been buried in the Old Cemetery since 1787, by which time pressure on space had become so acute that as many as a dozen superimposed burials had been made in some graves.

The New Town lies to the south of the Old Town. The boundary between the two is the broad street known as Na příkopé—meaning "on the moat", and recalling the ditch that used to defend the settlement until the 18th Century—and its continuation, Národní třída (National Avenue), that runs down to the Vltava by the National Theatre. The rather ponderous neo-Renaissance style of the theatre, completed in 1883, is typical of the architecture of much of Prague's New Town; for, although the latter district was originally laid out in 1348 by Charles IV, it has long been the centre of the city's commercial life, and it is therefore one area that did not escape extensive rebuilding in the 19th Century. Running south-east at right angles from Na příkopé is the geographical and commercial hub of today's Prague, Václavské náměstí (Wenceslas Square), built within the last century on what was originally a medieval horse market. It is not, in fact, a square but a long, wide avenue lined with hotels, cinemas, shops and restaurants. It sweeps uphill towards the large statue of Czechoslovakia's patron saint that gives the place its name.

Even if it cannot compare with the unique beauty of Prague's unchanged districts, the New Town has its own visual delights. There is the Municipal House, an elaborately decorated art nouveau edifice containing a concert hall, a ballroom, a restaurant and a café. And then there is the massive main railway station, built in similar style in the early 1900s for an age when express trains would come thundering into Prague en route for every major European city and even beyond, to the outskirts of Asia.

Prague's 20th-Century architecture is to be seen mainly in the suburbs. The city began to expand from its relatively small riverside site only in the early 19th Century, when the village of Karlín, two miles to the east, was absorbed. The expansion of industry led to the swallowing up of more and more outlying villages, and today these inner suburbs are spruce

Two children call up to friends living in the upper storeys of a 19th-Century tenement in Malá Strana. Although they lack privacy and sometimes suffer from the inconvenience of shared toilet facilities, such courtyard communities—with the traditional balconied buildings known as "pavlace"—provide sought-after accommodation because of their location close to the city centre.

places, full of tree-lined streets and villas with neat front gardens. But since the Second World War, outer suburbs have grown up in a ring round the entire city. They are as soulless as modern, high-density housing developments usually are. Apartment blocks rise 15 or 20 storeys from the ground, surrounded by the obligatory patch of grass planted with saplings; occasionally a piece of sculpture has been set up in an attempt to relieve the monotony of the view. Once upon a time, men did much better than this—a point that Prague makes more vividly than most cities.

But new high-rise blocks like those in the suburbs are nowhere to be seen in Prague's historical inner districts—and they never will be. The common bane of Western European cities—bulldozers smashing down old walls and cranes erecting ugly and more profitable new ones in their place—is unknown here, and the treatment of the valued ancient buildings is strictly controlled. For in 1971 the whole of central Prague—Old Town, New Town, Malá Strana and Hradčany—was declared an historical reserve, and the State Institute for the Reconstruction of Historic Towns and Monuments was given the job of taking care that it stayed beautiful. The decision was taken not a minute too soon.

The reserve is an area of about $3\frac{1}{2}$ square miles, densely packed with buildings crying out for preservation. One part of it, Hradčany, has always been well looked after because the castle and its immediate surroundings represent the greatest glories of this people, as well as the continuing centre of national government. Everything up there is immaculately in order. But Malá Strana to some degree, and the Old

Town and the New Town have suffered neglect over the ages. The removal of many properties from the care of loving owners into the possession of anonymous authorities did not help the situation, and by 1971 many buildings in the old quarters were badly in need of repair.

Much of the blame for the dilapidation can be placed on the climate that nature and man have combined to produce in Prague. Winters can be bitter in this part of the world, with frost damage to masonry that only shows up when the thaw has come in spring. And then there is the smog, which man has created by the use of coal. Motor traffic plays a part in putting up the dirty mist that hangs in a low sheet over the city most days of the year, but poor quality coal is the chief culprit; it is almost the only household fuel used by Praguers, and it is the corrosive gases from this stuff that have wrought havoc upon the old buildings of the city, quite as much as the frost and the damp. Down in the Old Town, bare stone is generally as black as pitch, and coloured plasterwork is stained with soot and other grime unless it has recently been renewed.

Part of the long-term plan to protect the historical reserve of old Prague was the building of a ring road to keep as much traffic as possible out of the city centre. Another measure was the strict application of rules about what can and cannot be done to alter the appearance of old buildings in Prague. At the top of three grades of listed buildings come the national cultural monuments, which may not be altered in any way. There are 19 such sites in Prague, including the entire castle complex and the Old Town Square, as well as individual structures such as the Charles Bridge.

Below the national monuments are the buildings graded as of regional importance, then those of purely local significance—and there are more than 2,000 Grade 2 (regional) buildings alone in this city. Restorations of Grade 2 structures are subject to the same restrictions as those in Grade 1, but work on them has a lower priority. Down at the level of Grade 3, however, certain interior modifications can be made, so that in time—probably a long time—a lot of the dwellings in the oldest parts of Prague will have modern amenities discreetly installed. Many of the 96,000 inhabitants of the town's old centre live in conditions of medieval austerity.

But it will be some time yet before the old houses in the historic core are modernized, because all resources are fully stretched in repairing the dilapidations of the past. You come across what looks like a building site in a courtyard of the Old Town, with piles of sand and cement dumped inside the gates, men hammering away at walls and women working cement mixers; they are, in fact, restoring some building that went up in the 16th Century and has come near to collapse 400 years later.

A minor hazard of walking around old Prague is the scaffolding which now surrounds so many of the old buildings there. It is uncommon to move more than a hundred yards in any direction without having to duck or side-step a network of steel erected along some wall, and in some cases

At Zabehlice, a modern suburb south-east of the city centre, high-rise apartment blocks tower on the skyline beyond a young family out on a springtime stroll among blossoming cherry trees. Prague's strict building regulations, aimed at protecting the character of the ancient inner districts, stipulate that large-scale housing schemes be erected only on the city's outskirts.

the scaffolding has stayed in place for years on end. The twin Gothic towers of the Týn Church disappeared behind this sheath of metal in 1974, not to reappear—according to the plan—until well into the 1980s. Meanwhile 15 masons slowly and painstakingly replace decayed stonework and mortar high above the Old Town Square.

There is at least no reluctance to make money available from the State to tackle all the restoration work that needs doing in old Prague. By the end of the 1970s there was an annual budget of 150 million crowns allotted to the historic reserve. The biggest problem is a shortage of labour. This is a common cry in Czechoslovakia as a whole, but in no area of the country's life is it as crucial as it is in the maintenance of Prague's great heritage from the past. There just aren't enough workmen, and particularly workmen with the necessary skills, to do all that ought to be done —and done quickly—if irreparable damage is not to occur. Even so, the officials of the State Institute make it clear that the last thing they would ever do is to call for outside help. National, and perhaps above all political, pride—together with the chronic shortage of hard currency for foreign exchange—forbids such an appeal.

Yet, even if the work is progressing at a painfully slow rate, the danger to Prague's architectural heritage is recognized and is being addressed. A hundred years from now, it will still be possible to amble slowly through the twisting streets of the Old Town and feel a continuity from the Middle Ages. It will still be possible to stroll on to the Charles Bridge towards evening in spring, when thrushes fill the air with song, and bats begin to skim about the eaves on Kampa Island, when the chestnut trees beside the river glow with candle-blossom and the lilacs cast their scent over the water. It will still be possible to watch the sun setting behind the high palisade of the castle, with the spires and buttresses and gargoyles of St. Vitus' soaring into the sky. Men will be very thankful that such things are possible because care was taken of the past in Prague.

In the Church of St. Nicholas in Prague's Old Town, the eight petal-like lobes of a crystal chandelier complement the octagonal shape of the cupola, designed

Legacies of the Habsburgs

in 1735 by Kilian Ignaz Dientzenhofer, one of the architects who helped to spread to central Europe the ornate baroque style that had originated in Italy.

Some of Prague's finest monuments are the direct legacy of Bohemia's long subjection to the Austrian rulers who, in the 17th and 18th Centuries, re-imposed Catholicism upon the Protestant Czechs; the churches that the Habsburgs lavishly endowed in the city's inner districts were first conceived as propaganda for a conquering faith. Craftsmen and artists came from all over Europe to work on the buildings and many—such as the renowned Dientzenhofer family of architects from Bavaria—settled in Prague. Their elaborate embellishments of new or remodelled baroque churches achieved dramatic effects: painted domes offer vistas of skies teeming with angels; polychrome statues of saints point the way to salvation; even the gilded swags of flowers and hosts of cherubs evoke the confidence of the Church triumphant.

Gilt, marble and stucco combine to produce the sumptuous effects of the Nativity Chapel in the Loreto Church, designed in 1734 by Jan Jiří Aichbauer.

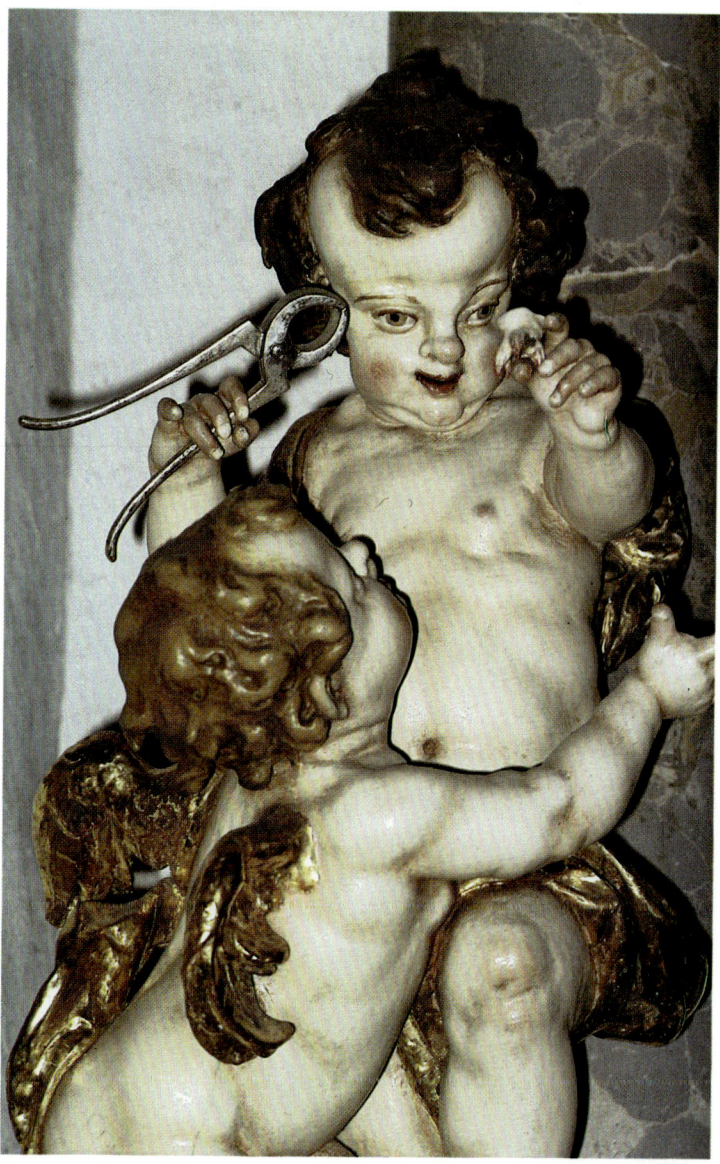

Pincers and a tooth honour a saint credited with power to relieve toothache.

In the 17th-Century Church of St. James, re-designed in 1736 by Jan Pánek, angels frame a painting of the saint's martyrdom located above the altar.

As if flushed by her exertions, an angel supports gilded garlands on the church's organ case. Vividly painted statues are characteristic of the baroque style.

A cherubic orchestra with realistic instruments adorns the organ gallery of St. Nicholas' Church in Malá Strana, begun in 1704 by Christoph Dientzenhofer.

Cloud-borne flights of painted saints and angels swirl within the 246-foot-high dome created for St. Nicholas' by Christoph's son, Kilian Ignaz, in 1753.

5
A Grand Devotion to the Arts

Every Sunday morning one church above all others in Prague is packed to the doors. St. James's, tucked away among the fairy-tale huddle of alleys and courtyards that encircles the Old Town Square, happens to be one of the noblest buildings in the city; originally built for John of Luxembourg, it was thoroughly reconstructed in baroque style during the late 17th Century. But the big attraction on Sundays is not the gorgeous plasterwork and painted ceilings of its interior, nor the solemn celebration of the Roman Catholic Mass, but the performances of choral or organ music—for which both architecture and liturgy provide the perfect setting.

Rising from a balcony over the west door of St. James's is a beautifully carved and gilded organ that has been played since 1705. A long tradition of excellence was begun at its keyboard by Friar Bohuslav Černohorský, who was musical director of St. James's from about 1739 to 1742 and the first of a succession of distinguished Prague organists and organ composers that has continued to this day. Each Sunday—even when the Mass is spoken rather than sung and no choir is present—crowds turn up at St. James's simply to hear the organist play.

But best attended of all are the mornings when the organist's voluntaries herald and conclude a large-scale choral work, especially if it is of Czech origin—such as one of the 76 Masses written by the 18th-Century Prague composer František Brixi. Then, the sound of rumbling Slav basses and skirling sopranos echoes around the gilded putti on the high vault of the church, reverberates along its tiers of arcaded galleries and finally slips out of the door, making this corner of the Old Town alive with music. There are 21 altars in St. James's and, at the foot of each, groups of people are sitting on the stone floor; the pews were filled long before the service began. Behind the pews, in the space in front of the west door, the congregation is standing crammed together like a soccer crowd. A few dozen of them go up to the high altar to receive Communion from the priests—but hundreds more remain motionless, listening raptly to the choir.

The crowded services at St. James's represent the merest fraction of Prague's cultural life, which—for a city of little more than a million people—is astonishingly rich and varied. My favourite guidebook to Prague proudly lists the Czech capital's 22 permanent theatres, three opera houses, two major symphony orchestras, 13 art galleries and 24 museums.

The great appetite of the Czechs for culture, especially their own, must in part be a product of their troubled history, since for long periods literature, music and the visual arts were almost the only available ways in which

A singing violinist entertains patrons at a restaurant on the outskirts of Prague. Musical performances, whether lofty or light, occupy a primary place in the life of the Czech capital, continuing a vigorous tradition that has its roots in the rich folk-music legacy of ancient Bohemia.

a subject people could assert its national identity and aspirations. This tendency frequently aroused the suspicion of alien overlords; and so, throughout the centuries, Czech artists—and in particular writers—have suffered bouts of official persecution.

Hus's reform of the native language—in which he and his fellow religious radicals wrote stirring theological treatises—marks the vigorous springtime of Czech literature, culminating in a magnificent vernacular translation of the Bible completed in 1593. But the Habsburg victory at the White Mountain in 1620 led also to the triumph in Bohemia of German culture and the German language; within 200 years Czech had almost ceased to exist as a literary medium and was spoken only by the peasantry.

The 19th-Century nationalist movement brought about a revival, drawing Czech writers into the orbit of pan-European literary movements, and at the beginning of the 20th Century there emerged two native-born authors who were to achieve worldwide fame: the Praguers Jaroslav Hašek, creator of *The Good Soldier Švejk*, and Franz Kafka (who wrote in German). Yet, it is symptomatic of the Czech writer's eternal predicament that Hašek and Kafka favoured, respectively, satire and allegory—literary forms that have been used throughout history to express obliquely sentiments that cannot, for safety's sake, be stated clearly. And, since the Communist takeover in 1948, literary repression has returned to Czechoslovakia with undiminished force. A present-day Czech writer must belong to the official Writers' Union, which expects him to toe the Party line as a condition of having his work published in his native land.

Music, being ostensibly a less "political" art form than literature, has fared rather better throughout Czech history. Although the Roman Catholic Church was largely responsible for suppressing the Czech language after 1620, its taste for elaborate settings of religious texts at least provided a stimulus to Czech music. The 18th Century, in particular, is littered with the names of Czech composers whose work was performed in churches and courts all over Europe; the list includes those "little masters"—such as Jan Stamic, Josef Mysliveček and František Benda—whose contribution to the mainstream of Western music has come to be fully appreciated only in recent years. However, the limited opportunities at home forced many composers to live and work abroad; the emigrant tradition was as strong among musicians as elsewhere in Czech society.

The development of a specifically Czech style of music—and of an audience for it—had to wait until the 19th Century, when, under the stimulus of nationalism, composers began to incorporate into their work the ancient folk songs of Bohemia and, occasionally, the four-square melodies of Hussite hymns. This period brought forth the two undisputed giants among Czech composers, Bedřich Smetana and Antonín Dvořák.

Today, the place of music in Czech national life seems assured. The fountainhead of all patronage is the State. The government pays the

A young Praguer scans the titles displayed in the window of one of Prague's 130 or so bookshops. Although all activities of the publishing industry are closely supervised by the Czech Ministry of Culture, the reading public's appetite for books remains voracious: queues form outside bookshops every Thursday morning, when newly published works go on sale.

wages of composers and performers, subsidizes concert tickets and maintains the traditionally high standards of performance by supporting numerous conservatories and music schools; at the same time, it tends to frown upon avant-garde music as an "élitist" activity incompatible with the ideals of a socialist state.

I know of no city other than Prague where you are more likely to see or hear, quite casually, physical evidence that music is vibrantly alive and of deep concern to the inhabitants. A newly varnished violin hangs to dry in the window of a tenement off Národní třída; the sound of a flute drifts from a room somewhere in the Old Town. One morning, in the course of a brief stroll through the little squares of Malá Strana, I heard four different instruments and two voices being put through their paces by unseen enthusiasts. And in the Old Town alone there seems to be a record shop on every corner, each of them stocked chiefly with classical music.

For music-lovers, Prague is inseparably associated with the "Prague Spring"—the international music festival that has been held in the city every year since 1946. The festival takes place during the three weeks following May 12, the anniversary of Smetana's death in 1884. It has become one of the major events in the European musical calendar, attracting ensembles and artistes from all over the world, although its backbone remains essentially Czech.

The opening concert is always held beneath the art nouveau-painted ceiling of the Smetana Hall in Prague's Municipal House. The President of the Republic sits in a flag-draped box, watched over by a few beefy security men lurking in the shadows behind. The Czech Philharmonic takes the platform before an audience as splendidly dressed as you will see in any concert hall nowadays. Everyone stands up for the national anthem, with its poignant opening based on the 19th-Century ballad *"Kde domov můj?"* ("Where is my Home?"). The remainder of the festival's first night always consists of a complete performance of Smetana's *Má Vlast* (My Country), a cycle of six symphonic poems that is rarely heard in its entirety outside its native land. Western audiences are generally familiar with only two of the poems: *Vltava* (as often as not referred to by its German name, *Moldau*) and *From Bohemia's Woods and Fields*.

The other four are *Tábor*, dedicated to the Hussite warriors; *Blaník*, named after the Bohemian mountain within which legend says these warriors still slumber, ready to respond to their nation's call; *Vyšehrad*, commemorating the fortress south of Prague that was the seat of the ancient Czech princes; and *Šárka*, evoking the legendary female warrior who led a revolt of Czech women against male domination. The six poems —in turn melancholy, triumphant, merry and elegiac—represent Smetana at his most lyrical, but it is, above all, their themes that appeal to Czech national pride and sentiment. No one who hears *Má Vlast* performed during the "Prague Spring" festival can fail to be moved by its transparent meaning for the audience.

The Czech taste for music-making, both professional and amateur, has long impressed outsiders. When the English musicologist Dr. Charles Burney returned home in 1772 from his extensive Continental travels, he concluded that the Czechs were "the most musical people of Germany [*sic*] or, perhaps, of all Europe". He had been particularly struck by the musical training given to children, noting that in one typical village small boys and girls between the ages of six and 11 were being taught the violin, the oboe and the bassoon, as well as being encouraged to practise on four clavichords owned by the local schoolmaster (who, as in many other villages, doubled as choirmaster).

Burney was writing shortly before Prague was to be visited by a supreme musical genius; in January 1787, Wolfgang Amadeus Mozart arrived in the city. The Austrian-born composer was by then 30 years old and an artist of prodigious range and achievement whose unique place in the history of music was already assured.

Mozart's musical gift was, of course, largely a miraculous freak, but from his earliest years outside influences had played upon his own instinctive talent—and some of these influences can be traced to the *émigré* Czech composers. Among the most important of these men was Jan Stamic, who from 1745 until his death in 1757 had been musical director to the court of Prince Karl Theodor, Elector Palatine, in the German city of Mannheim; Stamic's innovations, such as the development of the four-movement

In the Smetana Hall of Prague's Municipal House, the audience awaits the opening concert of the annual international music festival, the "Prague Spring".

symphony and the expressive "sighing" style of playing that he coaxed from the Mannheim orchestra, had a powerful influence on the musical language of late-18th-Century Europe.

Stamic's compatriot, Josef Mysliveček, spent most of the period between 1763 and 1781 in Italy, where he wrote more than 30 successful operas and earned the title *il divino Boemo* (the divine Bohemian); Mozart was a personal acquaintance of his. Brixi, the prolific writer of Masses, never left Prague and composed some 500 works there between the 1750s and his early death in 1771. Today, musicologists see Brixi as, above all, a man who led music into new areas of melodic invention and formal beauty that were later to be explored more fully by Mozart.

Mozart's visit to Prague was, in a sense, accidental. He had left his home town of Salzburg—and his unsympathetic employer, the town's Archbishop—in 1781 in order to try his fortunes in Vienna. Yet, despite a steady flow of commissions, and a busy career as a concert pianist, he found himself sliding ever deeper into debt. By 1787, therefore, he and his wife Constanze had decided to go to England, with thoughts of settling there for good if prospects seemed brighter than in Austria. Unfortunately, Mozart's father refused to take charge of his two grandchildren during their parents' absence, so the young couple could only make a brief exploratory trip to Prague instead.

They found the citizens enraptured by *The Marriage of Figaro*, which had recently been heard in Prague for the first time. At a ball Mozart attended melodies from the opera were played, and soon he was noting that: "Here they talk of nothing but *Figaro*; scrape, blow, sing and whistle nothing but *Figaro*; visit no opera but *Figaro* and eternally *Figaro*." On January 17 he and his wife went to a performance and were given a fantastic reception. Two days later he conducted the first performance of a symphony in D major that he had composed the year before; once again, his audience was enthralled—and so the work thereafter became known as the "Prague" Symphony.

Mozart was staying with Johann, Count Thun at his splendid baroque palace (now the British Embassy) in Malá Strana, but he saw a great deal of the pianist and composer František Dušek and his wife Josefa, a notable soprano. They had already met in Salzburg, but the friendship now deepened—fortunately both for Mozart's career and for the world of music. Dušek persuaded the impresario Pasquale Bondini to commission a new opera from Mozart—although Bondini probably needed little persuasion in view of the enormous financial success of *Figaro*.

By the time Mozart returned home that summer he had received an advance of a hundred ducats (about $7,000 in present-day values), which was rather more than he had been accustomed to. He thereupon began to compose *Don Giovanni*, to a libretto by Lorenzo da Ponte, the Italian poet who had previously supplied the text for *Figaro*. By an extra-

Elegantly dressed concert-goers exchange opinions after a performance in the Municipal House, the city's chief cultural centre. The audience for classical music in Prague is so wide that tickets are much sought after. A typical audience may include not only members of the professional and Party élite, but factory workers who benefit from subsidized ticket prices and block bookings made by their places of work.

ordinary coincidence, while Mozart was writing the music that would immortalize this classic story of the unprincipled rake, the most celebrated rake of all—Giovanni Giacomo Casanova—was compiling his memoirs in Count Valdštejn's chateau at Duchcov, 55 miles north-west of Prague where, as an act of charity, he had been made librarian in his old age. It is even possible that he had a hand in da Ponte's libretto for *Don Giovanni*.

Mozart returned to Prague in October 1787, his opera almost ready for its first performance. He and the pregnant Constanze lodged at the Three Golden Lions, an inn on Uhelný trh (Coal Market), a square in the Old Town; but they spent much of their time at Bertramka, the stuccoed villa belonging to the Dušeks in the south-western suburbs of the city. There, you can still see the spacious garden where Mozart sat for hours beneath the trees putting the finishing touches to *Don Giovanni*; he did not write the overture until the evening before the dress rehearsal. He certainly had some difficulty with the vocal score. Luigi Bassi, the notoriously temperamental Italian baritone who was to sing the title role, complained endlessly that he had not been given enough virtuoso music to perform, so Mozart was obliged to rewrite the duet "*La ci darem la mano*"—during which Don Giovanni successfully woos the peasant girl Zerlina—five times before Bassi was satisfied that it would show off his vocal talents to their best advantage.

But at last, on October 29, 1787, Mozart conducted the first performance of *Don Giovanni* at the Nostic Theatre, a magnificently decorated neo-classical building in the Old Town (now known as the Tyl Theatre, after the

140/ **A Grand Devotion to the Arts**

Czech music's great nationalistic revival in the 19th Century can be traced primarily to Bedřich Smetana (inset), who drew his special inspiration from the folk songs and traditions of his native land. During his 40-year career, he wrote numerous lyric dramas, choral works, symphonic poems and chamber pieces, but his most popular opus continues to be the comic opera "The Bartered Bride", a tale of peasant courtship and intrigue in a Bohemian village.

In a National Theatre production of "The Bartered Bride", cast members in rural Bohemian dress perform one of the folk dances that enliven the opera.

19th-Century Czech dramatist Josef Tyl). Once again, Prague was ecstatic—unlike Vienna, which gave the new opera a cool reception when it was first performed there six months later. But its success in Prague was enough to persuade Josef II, the Austrian Emperor, to appoint Mozart as chamber musician to the imperial court at a salary of 800 florins a year (the equivalent of $15,000 today).

Before returning south to Vienna, the Mozarts moved in with the Dušeks at Bertramka; and it was at about this time that Josefa collected the tiny wisp of the composer's hair that you can still just about detect—with the aid of a magnifying glass—lying in a showcase at the villa. She was certainly intent on wringing more music out of Mozart, and locked him in the summerhouse one day on pain of not being released until he had written a concert aria especially for her; the composer retaliated with the fearsomely difficult "Bella mia fiamma".

Mozart was to return to Prague only once more, in 1791, for the first performance of another opera, La Clemenza di Tito, commissioned for the coronation of the Austrian Emperor Leopold II as King of Bohemia. Mozart wrote the work in a mere 18 days, conducted it at the royal festivities and then departed. Within a few weeks he was dead of heart failure and the Viennese put him in a pauper's grave. In Prague, thousands turned out for a special Requiem Mass at the Church of St. Nicholas in Malá Strana, during which Josefa Dušek sang solos from the organ loft. "My Praguers," Mozart had said after the first night of Don Giovanni, "understand me."

During the two hundred years since, that same understanding has been extended to almost every great name in European music, as composers and performers have visited Prague on the international concert circuit. Some—including Carl Maria von Weber, who directed the Prague Opera from 1813 to 1816, and Gustav Mahler, who was second conductor at the German Provincial Theatre from 1885 to 1886—made their home there for a while. At the same time, the music schools of Prague continued to train Czech composers who were to achieve worldwide reputations. Leoš Janáček (1854-1928) employed his genius for vocal writing and his deep knowledge of Czech folk music to create operas of enduring popularity that range in mood from rustic comedy to austere tragedy. Bohuslav Martinů (1890-1959) spent half his adult life in France and the United States of America, but never forgot his homeland, to whose tragic history he paid moving tribute in his symphonic poem Memorial to Lidice. But the most celebrated of all the Prague-trained composers, whose presence still looms large in the city's musical life, were Smetana and Dvořák.

Bedřich Smetana was a curious paradox. He was born in 1824 in the ancient Bohemian town of Litomyšl, the son of a brewery manager, and from infancy until after the completion of his musical studies in Prague he spoke little but German. He associated himself closely with the Czech nationalist movement of the 19th Century—which is one reason why he is today held in such high popular esteem in Czechoslovakia. Yet, even at the age of 36 he was forced to admit "I cannot express myself adequately, nor write correctly, in Czech", and the native tongue was to cause him difficulty throughout his life.

At the age of 19 Smetana was appointed music master to the children of Leopold, Count Thun—a member of the same Prague noble family that had given hospitality to Mozart—but resigned after three years to try his luck as a concert pianist. His tour of Bohemia was a flop and he was reduced to scraping a living as a piano teacher. During the 1848 Prague insurrection against Austrian rule, Smetana—an ardent supporter of the insurgents—wrote stirring revolutionary songs and is said to have helped man the barricades on the Charles Bridge.

The insurrection failed, but Smetana's fortunes began to mend. Married in 1849, he opened a music school in the Old Town Square, which soon attracted pupils from among the Prague nobility. But Prague's indifference to his compositions—coupled perhaps with his disenchantment over the future of Czech nationalism—caused the dispirited Smetana to emigrate in 1856 to Göteborg in Sweden, where he opened another successful music school. "I shall probably make my future here," he wrote. "Prague did not wish to recognize me, therefore I have left her."

Within five years, however, homesickness began to prevail over wounded pride and the news of recent developments in Prague supplied a further incentive for his return. The repressive political climate had begun to ease and plans were being laid for a national theatre that would be exclusively Czech in outlook. When Smetana heard that it was to be used for opera as well as drama, he decided to go back. In 1862 he became chorus master of the newly founded Hlahol Choral Society and, four years later, principal conductor of the Czech Opera—two positions that allowed him to give full rein to his musical nationalism. They also exposed him to counter-attack; after one of his concerts, Smetana noticed that the German music critics of Prague savaged the performance while their Czech counterparts praised it.

Paradoxically, his first opera on a patriotic theme, *The Brandenburgers in Bohemia*—first performed in 1866, to considerable popular acclaim, at Prague's Provisional Theatre (a stop-gap structure used until the National Theatre's permanent home could be completed)—was censured in some quarters for its supposedly "Germanic" musical idiom; a charge that was to be often repeated throughout the composer's career. But this was a purely musical judgment; Smetana was politically immovable. He once wrote to the Czech cellist František Neruda: "You know what a hard struggle our nation is having to wage for its sealed and sacred rights . . . with the present government, a government that would dearly like to throw *all* the nations of Austria into one pot—that of Germanization."

Flowers bearing ribbons with the Czech national colours adorn the tomb of composer Antonín Dvořák in Prague's ancient Vyšehrad Cemetery. Like his older contemporary Bedřich Smetana, who is buried nearby, Dvořák devoted himself to the establishment of a specifically Czech style of music. His symphonic and choral works had won him an international reputation by the time of his death in 1904 at the age of 63.

Profiled in a cartoon, the eponymous hero of "The Good Soldier Švejk", the satirical novel written by Jaroslav Hašek and brought out between 1920 and 1923, radiates the earthy good humour that has made him the international archetype of the little man who survives in the face of uncontrollable events—and a particular symbol of Czech resistance to oppression. The print—one of a series by the book's original illustrator, Josef Lada—decorates a wall of the well-known beer parlour Ú Kalicha (At the Chalice), which owes its present-day popularity to its frequent mention in Hašek's book.

However, a milestone in the history of Czech music was soon to be reached. A few months after the opening of *The Brandenburgers*, Smetana's new opera, *The Bartered Bride*—a light-hearted comedy set in the Bohemian countryside and telling of the intrigues surrounding the marriage of a village girl—succeeded even beyond its composer's expectation. In spite of a disastrous first performance (held on one of the hottest days of the year, when few citizens felt inclined to incarcerate themselves in a stuffy theatre) the Praguers soon became as fond of it as they had been of *Figaro* 80 years before, and for much the same reason; it was full of catchy tunes that they could hum and whistle in the street. *The Bartered Bride* was, without doubt, Smetana's most successful opera; yet the composer himself always viewed it rather coolly. He once described it as "only a toy. I composed it not out of vanity but out of spite, because after *The Brandenburgers* I was accused of being Wagnerian and not capable of doing anything in a lighter, national style."

The beginning of construction work on the new National Theatre was at last drawing near, an event that was to have far more than simply dramatic and musical significance. On May 16, 1868—the feast-day of St. John of Nepomuk—a great procession of Czechs wound its way through Prague to the theatre site on the east bank of the Vltava, and there, as the foundation-stone was laid, Smetana proclaimed: "Music is the life of the Czechs." That evening, the composer conducted the first performance of his opera *Dalibor*, a moving account of the imprisonment and eventual death of a medieval Czech knight who led a peasant revolt against baronial tyranny. The work was enthusiastically acclaimed—although in some quarters the old "Wagnerian" taunt was revived—and Smetana himself always considered it to be his greatest achievement.

Now at the height of his powers, he was composing furiously, drawing more and more for inspiration upon the ancient myths of his people. By the time work on the National Theatre was well under way, he had completed yet another opera, *Libuše*, about the legendary Czech princess of pagan times who stood on a bare hill overlooking the Vltava and prophesied that a great city would one day arise there.

Then tragedy struck. One day in July 1874, while out duck-shooting, Smetana began to go deaf. By October he could not hear a thing and the doctors could do nothing for him. Yet, a mere month after being locked into a world without sound, he was strolling past a sawmill on a little tributary of the Vltava when he was seized with the idea of writing a musical portrait of Prague's river—an idea that grew into *Vltava*, the second symphonic poem in the *Má Vlast* cycle.

Smetana's programme note to the fifth poem of that cycle, *Tábor*, suggests what was going on inside that sad, soundless head: "The work tells of strong will, victorious fights, constancy and endurance and stubborn refusal to yield . . . ." He still attended opera, but usually left after the first act, unable to bear the frustration of merely watching the singers' gestures. In this condition he saw *Libuše* performed at the opening of the National Theatre in June 1881.

Two months later the new building was gutted by fire and Prague opened a public subscription so that the theatre should rise again without delay. Within two years, aided by contributions from thousands of ordinary Czechs, the rebuilding was completed and *Libuše* was once again staged on the opening night. But by then Smetana's deafness had driven him to insanity. He was placed in the Prague lunatic asylum and died there in 1884, leaving behind a body of music that would always stir his people in both good times and bad.

Libuše is still the Czechs' choice of opera for any great national occasion; and today, at the Smetana Museum a few yards below the Charles Bridge —housed in what used to be the Prague waterworks— they attend to his memory well. Tapes of his music play softly there all the time, so that you can inspect the score of *Má Vlast* with the strains of *Vltava* in your ears while the river itself rushes past the open window of the exhibition room.

Dvořák, 17 years younger than Smetana, had a much less tortured life, although his origins and early struggles were similar. Another boy from the Bohemian countryside, son of a butcher-cum-innkeeper, he was playing the violin alongside his father in the village band before he was 12. At that point the young Dvořák, who spoke nothing but Czech, was sent to another school in order to learn German, which in the Bohemia of the 1850s was vital if you wished to live anything other than the life of a peasant. His father had hopes that he would become some urban bureaucrat, but Dvořák was already set on a musical career and, at the age of 16, with an uncle's backing, he got himself into the Prague Organ School.

He was not a particularly distinguished pupil, although his teachers thought he might make a passable organist and choirmaster. In fact he became a professional viola player in a restaurant orchestra, and later played in the orchestra pit of the Czech Opera—which meant that he regularly performed under Smetana's baton. He began composing chamber music and symphonies, but burnt most of them as soon as they were finished because he considered them rubbish.

The experience of playing in the string section for the first performance of *The Bartered Bride* inspired Dvořák to make an attempt at opera and he wrote a work called *King and Collier*; like Smetana's opera, it concerns a misunderstanding between rustic lovers—in this case, a charcoal-burner's daughter and her sweetheart. Smetana gave the overture a public hearing but declared that the remainder of the opera, although full of genius, was unplayable. Dvořák, a dogged as well as a fertile man, thereupon rewrote every note—producing, in effect, an entirely new opera under the old name—and in 1874 it was performed with great success.

The composer was by now married (to a contralto) and had caught the eye of the Austrian Commission for the State Music Prize. The Commission awarded generous grants to musicians who had been born within the Austrian Empire; and one of the Commission's judges was Johannes Brahms, who was impressed by Dvořák's talent. From that contact onwards Dvořák's star began to rise, never to set. A long string of chamber works flowed from his pen, winning for him a comfortable income and the State Prize three years running.

Somehow or other, amid the demands of composition and a growing family, Dvořák still found time to pursue his hobbies as pigeon-fancier and railway enthusiast. Whenever he was served pigeon at a meal, he would get up and leave the table in distress. And he once shook his head sadly when a prospective son-in-law, who had been dispatched to Prague's main station in order to check the number of a new express train, returned with the number of the tender instead of that of the locomotive. "And this," said Dvořák to his daughter, "is the sort of man you want to marry!"

In 1884 Dvořák paid the first of several visits to England—where he soon acquired an enthusiastic following—and, eight years later, he was enticed across the Atlantic. Mrs. Jeannette Thurber, wife of a wealthy New York grocer, had decided to found a National Conservatory of Music—part of her campaign to become the foremost patron of American musical life—and was looking for a director who would give it the right touch of class. A friend suggested two names, Sibelius and Dvořák. Since the Finn was then only 28, and the Czech was 50, she made her pitch for Dvořák. For a long time he declined, but Mrs. Thurber was as determined as she

No writer has better expressed the sense of tragic alienation than Franz Kafka, a Praguer of German-Jewish extraction, born in 1883 and shown here in a photograph taken in 1923—the year before his death at the age of 40. Kafka's disturbing tales of menace and human isolation are haunted by the claustrophobic atmosphere that he discerned in the city's Old Town, where he lived for the greater part of his life.

was wealthy and, eventually, in September 1892, Dvořák arrived in New York with his wife, two of his six children and a two-year contract. He never really took to New York itself—apart from the opportunities it offered for observing trains at the railway bridge spanning the Harlem River and for watching the pigeons in Central Park; but shortly after his arrival he discovered the small town of Spillville, Iowa, which was largely inhabited by Czech immigrants, and there, where he and his family spent a four-month vacation, he was happy indeed. He also met the black singer and composer Thacker Burleigh, a teacher at the Conservatory, who introduced him to the riches of Negro folk song. And he read a Czech translation of Longfellow's *The Song of Hiawatha* which entranced him.

Inspired by this amalgam of experiences, Dvořák wrote his Symphony in E Minor ("From the New World"), which was first performed at Carnegie Hall on December 16, 1893. The *New York Herald*'s review was condescending, but otherwise the response was favourable, if not exactly ecstatic. More importantly, the symphony was enough to confirm Mrs. Thurber's judgment that she had chosen the right guiding hand for her American musical dream. She tried to induce Dvořák to write an opera on the Hiawatha theme, but failed. She did manage to persuade him to return to New York—after five months' leave in Bohemia—for a second term as director of her Conservatory, hoping that he would produce something even more American than the "New World" Symphony. Again, failure—although that second trip did inspire the Cello Concerto in B Minor, which Dvořák wrote in his East 17th Street Manhattan apartment and conducted at its first performance in London in 1896.

After his final farewell to New York in 1895, Dvořák settled down at his country home in Vysoká, a village south of Prague. There, he would rise early and go for a walk, before playing the organ at 6 o'clock Mass in the village church. After breakfast he would compose for a few hours, then stroll again through the woods. His evenings were frequently spent at the village inn, playing cards and telling the locals about America. But he resumed teaching in Prague and made several European concert tours. His sorrow at the death of his old friend and patron Brahms in 1897 stopped the flow of composition for a while. Dvořák took Brahms's place on the Commission for the State Music Prize and in 1901 became the first musician ever to be made a life member (the equivalent of a British life peer) of the upper house of the Austrian Parliament—an honour that Bedřich Smetana, as an overt supporter of Czech nationalism, could never have been offered.

Dvořák was now a grand old man of European music and he celebrated by writing *Rusalka*, the ninth of his operas—the only one ever to achieve an enduring reputation, even in his own land, where it competes in popularity with *The Bartered Bride*. This variation on the Undine legend—the water-nymph who is allowed to become human on condition that she never speaks—was not the composer's last work; but by the time Prague first heard it, in March 1901, Dvořák was a sick man nearing the end of his life. A chill caught while visiting the Prague engine sheds finally caused his death, on May Day, 1904.

Although, unlike Smetana, Dvořák had rarely displayed his patriotism outside the sphere of music, his countrymen buried him near Smetana's grave in the cemetery at Vyšehrad, which has always been reserved for the most illustrious of Czechs. Later regimes have been less kind towards Dvořák's memory; the historian Zdeněk Nejedlý, who served as Czech Minister of Culture under Gottwald (and who, interestingly, was a native of Litomyšl, Smetana's birthplace) began a campaign in the early 1900s to enhance Smetana's reputation at the expense of Dvořák's, allegedly because the latter was insufficiently "patriotic". But this disagreeable episode could not obscure the truth about Smetana and Dvořák—*both* were great composers and great patriots.

The diversity of attitude among Czechs towards Austrian rule is fairly demonstrated by the lives of Smetana and Dvořák: the former being resentful, the latter often complaisant. "What have either of us to do with politics?" Dvořák once wrote to his music publisher in Vienna, "Let's be happy that we can consecrate our services to the fine arts alone!"

A similarly sharp contrast of attitude towards the alien power is detectable in the Prague writers Jaroslav Hašek and Franz Kafka, who were born within a few weeks of each other in 1883. But, whereas Kafka came from the German-Jewish community that had long been established in the city, Hašek—the son of a drunken schoolmaster—was pure Czech.

Hašek's anarchic tendencies showed themselves early in life, when he engaged in adolescent rebellion against Austrian authority, throwing stones through the windows of government buildings here, damaging a Habsburg eagle there, and, from time to time, getting caught by the police. Had there not been Austrians, Hašek would undoubtedly have found other targets; he was disorderly by nature, habitually consorted with gipsies and tramps, and was a great practical joker (he once feigned a suicide attempt by threatening to jump off the Charles Bridge and, for his pains, was briefly incarcerated in a lunatic asylum). Hašek was both metaphorically and literally a thorough Bohemian.

Practically his sole asset was his literary talent, which he exercised from at least the age of 19, when he managed to get himself sacked from his first steady job, as a bank clerk. The writing of copious short stories and articles constituted the only consistent thread in his life thereafter; he wrote steadily through a brief flirtation with the anarchist movement, a disastrous marriage, enlistment in the Imperial Army at the beginning of the First World War, confinement in Russian prisoner-of-war camps, and even two years as a Soviet commissar in various small Russian towns.

Actors of Prague's experimental Laterna Magica (Magic Lantern) troupe present their own brand of theatre—mime co-ordinated with filmed images projected on to the screen that serves as backdrop. Originally assembled for the Czechoslovak Pavilion at the 1958 Expo world exhibition in Brussels, the company continues to explore the potentialities of multi-media performance from the permanent home of its own theatre in Prague's New Town district.

/149

Four film posters evoking a variety of moods exemplify the range and sophistication of the widely admired Czech tradition of graphic design. Commissioned by the national film distribution agency from well-known artists, such posters are considered by both public and designers as an art form in their own right.

In 1920, Hašek returned to Prague—now the capital of the newly independent Republic of Czechoslovakia—but remained just as much a misfit as he had been when Bohemia was a vassal state. Branded as a Bolshevik and a bigamist (he had brought back another wife from Russia), he drank himself steadily downhill until his death in 1923. But two years before that, he had begun to write *The Good Soldier Švejk*; and for this one book Jaroslav Hašek passed into literary history.

He had first used the title in 1911 in a series of comic tales published in the satirical magazine *Karikatury*, which was edited by the artist Josef Lada—whose brilliant illustrations were to become inseparable from Švejk when the character was reincarnated in book form. The good soldier who first raised his amiably ugly mug in newsprint was only a sketch of the character who was to achieve international fame between hard covers after Hašek himself had been through the toils of war.

The reason why the novel, although unfinished, became a popular success the moment it appeared, and has remained a steady best seller in many languages ever since, is that Švejk represents the "little man" of any nation or era who manages to avoid being smothered by oppression, whether military, political or bureaucratic. It is almost incidental that he happens to be a fat little dog-dealer from Prague, already discharged once from the Imperial Army for "idiocy", who is reconscripted as an officer's batman in 1914, when the Austrian Archduke Franz Ferdinand is assassinated and Europe goes to war.

Švejk is a born survivor. He appears to be foolish, but isn't at all. He agrees with absolutely every word his superiors utter, but quietly undermines their authority by incompetence, artfulness or plain bloody-mindedness. He declares his patriotic anxiety (that is, his servile obligation) to get to the battle-front as fast as possible, but everything he does contrives to delay his actual appearance in the trenches. Švejk is a touchstone for all the ragamuffin underdogs of this world. In the process of winning our sympathy, he makes the mighty Austro-Hungarian Empire and its Imperial Army a laughing-stock.

By contrast, there isn't a smile, let alone a laugh, in anything that Franz Kafka wrote; and the ominous clouds that drift from the pages of his novels and short stories have at least as much to do with the ghetto complex of the Jew as with the facts of life in a Prague that was riddled with police informers. His mother's family were scholarly and rabbinical, but it was his father Hermann, a tough, prosperous merchant and property owner, who towered terribly over Kafka's life and contributed further to his sense of powerlessness and isolation. One of the writer's earliest and most searing memories was of a night when his infant crying so irritated Hermann that he took Franz from his bed and locked the child out on the balcony that runs around the courtyard of so many buildings in the Old Town of Prague. This incident occurred when the family was living on

Romance: "How to Awaken Princesses"

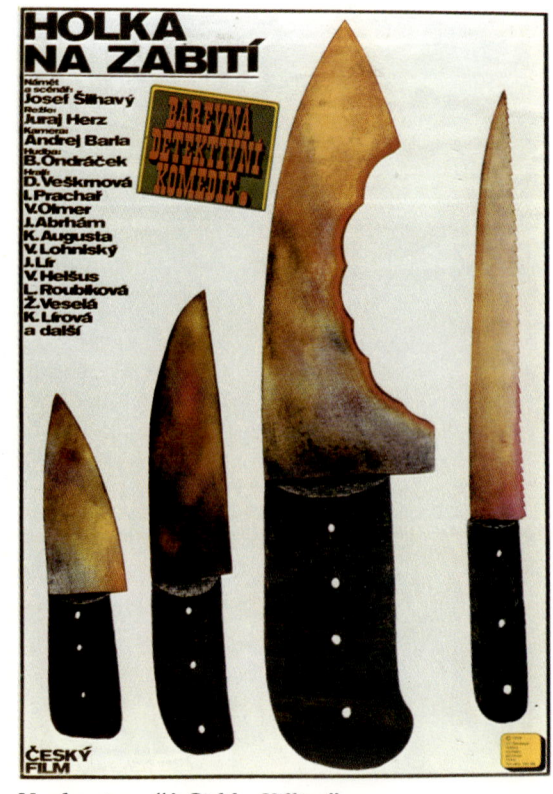

Murder story: "A Girl for Killing"

British musical comedy: "Oliver"

Melodrama: "Broken Glass for Eva"

Kaprova, a street not far from Pařížská, where the family later moved and where Kafka also rented a room and a study.

Although Kafka's work belongs to German literature, he was a Czech citizen, and Prague was always his home town, in spite of regular wanderings abroad. He attended the German grammar school in the Old Town Square, and obtained his doctorate in law at the Charles-Ferdinand University. His first job after qualifying was with the Prague office of an Italian insurance company; and from 1908 until his premature retirement in 1922 on grounds of ill health he worked for a government insurance organization. He died in 1924 at a tuberculosis sanatorium outside Vienna, but his body was brought home for burial in the Jewish cemetery at Strasnice, a Prague suburb.

Kafka, like Hašek, would probably have been a misfit anywhere, but it was Prague, at a particular point in its history, that formed him—and he was at odds with most of the things about the city (except for a few friendships with Praguers, such as the novelist Max Brod, his eventual biographer). One day in 1911 he described Prague's suburbs in his diary as "the miserable dark edge of the city that is furrowed like a great ditch". He could often be seen walking through the city's parks with cotton wool stuffed into his ears to keep out all sounds.

Kafka's major novels, for all their meticulous clarity of language, are proverbially difficult to analyse. Indeed, they have been described as possessing "the most obscure lucidity in the history of literature". Their author, with his despairing sense of alienation from God, from humanity and from the world at large, can scarcely be called "political" in the narrow sense; yet, the fearful predicament of Land Surveyor K.—who, in *The Castle*, goes to take up a post in a strange village, but never succeeds in making contact with his supposed employer—and even more so that of Joseph K., the bank-clerk hero of *The Trial*—who is arrested, tried and executed on a charge that is never specified—surely reflect in part the nightmarish political atmosphere of certain places and moments in European history. Kafka wrote during the decline and aftermath of empire from a satellite city, where Czech and German were suspicious of each other—especially after Czechoslovak independence in 1918, when their relationship was abruptly reversed—and where, as always, the Jew was made uneasy by the Gentile.

Whatever Kafka's meaning, his novels have consistently incurred the displeasure of totalitarian regimes. In Czechoslovakia, they were banned during both the Nazi occupation and the early years of the Communist regime. In 1968 Kafka's works were briefly allowed to circulate again and a plaque was placed on the wall of his birthplace in the Old Town, where a restaurant functions beneath a sign advertising "Pivo, Vino, Kava, Čaj, Limonady, Mineralky" (Beer, Wine, Coffee, Tea, Lemonade, Mineral Water). And that was the only way of identifying the spot when I last visited it, for Kafka's books had once again become unavailable in Prague and the plaque had been taken away—although you could see quite clearly where it had once hung.

The fate of Kafka's work is also shared by that of the best of Czechoslovakia's present-day writers; which is scarcely surprising, since so much of it provided implicit support for the political liberalization that flowered for a short span in 1968. Milan Kundera had written *The Joke*, a novel about a young man who is morally corrupted by socialism. Josef Škvorecký's *The Cowards* had scandalized the Party because it portrayed the soldiers of the Red Army as neither better nor worse than any other nation's cannon fodder. In *The Axe*, the novelist Ludvík Vaculík examined the contemporary implications of the age-old tension between the successful city slicker and his immovably provincial relatives, one of whom explains his reluctance to join the Party—or indeed anything else fashionable—with the trenchant words: "This era favours the stupider half of men. Let it do so, but without me."

There are others besides Kundera and Vaculík whose works are unobtainable in the bookshops of Prague. Some fled the country after 1968. Others stayed behind, but have only managed to eke out an existence by taking on the least enviable manual jobs, as window-cleaners, street-sweepers and nightwatchmen. Writing of their kind still goes on in Prague, but it is only available in *samizdat*, a euphemism (meaning literally "self-published" in Russian) used throughout Eastern Europe to refer to clandestine circulation.

In spite of the obstacles that have been placed in the way of freedom of expression, Prague still manages to display a high level of artistic achievement and appreciation in many spheres. Drama flourishes almost as vigorously as music; in addition to the city's permanent theatres there are numerous, intermittent "fringe" ventures. During an average week it is possible for Praguers to see plays not only by a cross-section of East European dramatists but also by classic Western writers. The names of Shakespeare, Ibsen, Brecht, Anouilh and Shaw crop up regularly, as well as lighter offerings, such as J. M. Barrie comedies and Richard Rodgers musicals. Considering that the market for Czech translations must be one of the smallest in the world, this is a remarkable state of affairs; even though it is nowadays partly the result of the official muzzling of many of Czechoslovakia's finest native playwrights. Theatre directors have learnt to resist the temptation to put on plays that the authorities might consider to be unduly "pessimistic" or that contain sentiments that might be construed as a comment, however oblique, on the political situation in present-day Czechoslovakia.

The most distinctive of the city's theatre companies, the famous "Black Theatre of Prague", has managed to avoid such difficulties and, in fact,

Visiting the Julius Fučik Amusement Park in the north of the city, a gipsy couple—members of Czechoslovakia's half-million or so Romany population—join several other pleasure-seekers in an impromptu dance to the compelling rhythms of a nearby band. The spacious park is a favourite leisure centre for Praguers of all ages, numbering among its attractions a sports stadium, a planetarium and several cinemas.

spends much of its time on tour in the West. Against a black backdrop, and assisted by spectral lighting and costumes, its players re-enact the mysterious legends of Old Prague—the Emperor Rudolf II's obsession with alchemy, or the Rabbi Löw's creation of the Golem. Another Prague speciality is children's theatre, which runs the gamut from fairy-tales through Czech legend to modern puppetry. A couple of the department stores in the New Town have children's theatres on their premises, so that parents can leave their offspring to be amused for an hour or so in safety while they get on with their shopping.

Czech film-making first seized the attention of the world in the 1960s, when the studio at Barrandov, in the south-western outskirts of Prague, began its succession of "New Wave" films, made by directors who included Miloš Forman and Jiří Menzel. Productions such as Menzel's Oscar-winning *Closely Observed Trains*—concerning the exploits of a shy young railwayman as a lover and as a member of the Czech Resistance during the Second World War—demonstrated a lyrical approach to cinema, as well as an engagingly sly sense of humour. Far removed from the grandiose epics that all too often flow from the studios of the Eastern bloc—and from those of the West as well—the new Czech films took an almost perverse delight in contemplating humanity at its most ridiculous and droll. At the same time, with the brief, pungent cartoons that also emanated from Barrandov, the art of the animated film took its first appreciable step forward since Walt Disney made his first feature.

Innovation has, in fact, always been a hallmark of any Czech who has a professional movie-camera at hand. It was Prague that invented the combination of mime and film that became the talk of the Brussels world exhibition in 1958. Every night the Laterna Magica gives a performance at its theatre on the Národní třída, sometimes playing for laughs, sometimes full of pathos, and occasionally making bitter little political references to the past; but always brilliantly ingenious, as the mime artists on stage synchronize their movements with the film projected on to screens behind and around them on three sides.

It would be quite misleading to imply that every Praguer has sophisticated tastes in entertainment. Pop music, for example, has a wider following than many Westerners might suppose. If there was one name instantly recognizable to anyone in Czechoslovakia at the end of the 1970s, it was that of the singer Karel Gott, whose photograph appeared in practically every record shop in Prague; and there are many other performers, such as Helena Vondračkova, who are quite as competent—and as popular—as their counterparts in the West.

On summer days a favourite place of resort for Praguers is the Julius Fučik Amusement Park (named after a Communist writer murdered by the Gestapo), north of the city centre, where there are dodgem cars,

Ferris wheels, miniature railways and hot-dog stalls. Amid all the fun of the fair is an open-air stage where pop groups regularly give free performances.

There are only two differences between what you can see there on a Sunday afternoon in June, and what you might witness among similar surroundings in, say, Cleveland or Croydon. One is the composition of the audience, which in Prague does not consist solely of young people, but rather a complete cross-section of the population, from infants to the elderly; a couple of pensioners might occupy a seat alongside two teenagers holding hands, while in the row behind sits a middle-aged man who looks as if he might be somebody important in a bank.

The other difference lies in the conduct of the performers on stage. The lyrics of their songs are as full of "lu-u-u-v" and titillation as anything ever mouthed by the Rolling Stones; yet, a little foot-stamping and head-shaking is as far as they go. There are no indelicate gestures with electric guitars, no suggestive thrusts of those tightly trousered hips.

An equally wide range of audience is visible at classical concerts and at the opera. The subsidized tickets are ridiculously inexpensive by Western standards, so almost everyone can afford to go. Parents give their small children a first taste of opera by taking them to see *Rusalka*, with breathtakingly imaginative sets by talents such as Josef Svoboda (the Czech stage designer who, beginning in the 1960s, organized his time between Prague and the theatres of the West), in the exquisite white and gold setting of the Smetana Theatre, the loveliest opera house I know.

Yet, for an opera-lover, the most thrilling experience Prague has to offer is to sit, preferably during the "Prague Spring" festival, within the green walls of the Tyl Theatre and listen to the music of *Don Giovanni* rising through the gilded tiers of seats to the narrow, oval roof, just as it was heard on that triumphant first night almost 200 years ago. And for those few hours in Prague you will know that magic still exists.

School for Champions

While a coach prepares the balance beam for practice (left) one young pupil rehearses her floor routine and another works on the asymmetric bars (background).

Gymnastic training in Czechoslovakia is a prime example of the way the state education system encourages children to develop their special talents from an early age. Prague's gymnastics school, one of six sports schools in the city, selects promising pupils at the age of eight for a seven-year course of intensive training. The success of the undertaking is evident in the consistently high ranking of Czech gymnasts in world events.

Girls follow the four parts of the programme for the women's competition working on floor exercises (choreographed to music), the balance beam, the vaulting horse, and the high-and-low asymmetric bars, on which so many gymnasts from Eastern Europe have displayed strength and grace. Highly gifted pupils are able to train with national coaches at the ultramodern Strahov sports complex, where these pictures were taken.

In a warming-up exercise before apparatus work students extend arms and legs to stretch the muscles and make them more supple. The girls work on the regulation surface specified for international competitions: a carpeted floor of sponge rubber between layers of plywood.

Before starting to practise on the asymmetric bars, a pupil applies chalk to her palms for a firm grip.

With perfect balance and fierce concentration, a talented young gymnast maintains a classic position on the balance beam, nearly four feet above floor level.

Using a video set—here being adjusted by a technician—two national coaches based at the gymnasium analyse a girl's performance on the asymmetric bars.

Under the guidance of a coach, a gymnast swings through a basic handstand position during a fluid movement that will transfer her from the high bar to the low.

Adopting a gymnastic pose even for writing, a student records in her class training book the apparatus work she has completed during the session. Her varied programme is drawn up by the coach to peak at the main competition time in early summer. Children at the gymnastics school practise for two to three hours a day, but are nevertheless expected to maintain a good all-round standard in their academic work.

6

Under the Communist Yoke

I am climbing the steps of a rather forbidding building, adorned with art nouveau statuary, that frowns across a small square in the Old Town of Prague. Two black limousines are parked outside, a sure sign that this is a place frequented by V.I.P.s. It is, in fact, Prague's functioning Town Hall and, as such, the headquarters of a gigantic monopoly that dominates almost every aspect of the city's life. Ever since 1948, when the Communists came to power in Czechoslovakia, the only civic affairs not managed from this building have been those for which the national government assumes responsibility: the police force, for example, or the major industries. Unlike Western cities, Prague does not have semi-autonomous bodies to run its transport system or gas and electricity supply; the city council, officially termed the Prague National Committee, directly controls these services, as well as others—such as taxis, construction work and theatres—that the West is accustomed to leaving in private hands.

I have come to the Town Hall to find out how Prague works. Therefore I have made an appointment to interview the *primátor*, the city's Lord Mayor, whose office dates back to the incumbency of one Pavel Zipansky z Dražic in 1558. But first I must have my credentials checked at the reception desk by elderly men in grey denims who display a red star on their caps and red armbands bearing the initials Z.S. They are members of the Závodní Stráž—literally "Factory Guard"—a body that has no counterpart in the West but which in Czechoslovakia supplies, for such jobs as this, a corps of men and women unquestionably loyal to prevailing Communist Party discipline.

The Závodní Stráž had its origins in the bands of armed factory guards recruited under the direction of the Communist-dominated Ministry of the Interior during the uncertain period immediately after the Second World War. In February 1948, President Edvard Beneš was expected to dissolve parliament and call new elections; when Prime Minister Klement Gottwald urged his fellow-Communists to positive action, these guards undoubtedly tilted the political balance in their leader's favour by occupying the factories of Prague. Four days later the President gave Gottwald the mandate to form a government and the Communist Party became the undisputed power in Czechoslovakia.

One of the guards now leads me through the Town Hall's rabbit-warren of corridors, which are as dreary as most municipal interiors, whether in the East or the West. Eventually, however, he throws open some impressive doors and ushers me into a grand chamber. At a long table, several places

At a street intersection in the north of the city gratings in the road-bed belch clouds of steam from the underground pipes that deliver heat to Prague's older buildings. More recent construction uses natural gas—largely imported from the Soviet Union—supplemented by brown coal mined in northern Bohemia and Moravia.

have been set with glasses of *slivovice* (plum brandy—at 9.30 a.m.!), cups of coffee and plates of biscuits. The primátor enters the room and sits down opposite me, flanked by two assistants. I have already been warned that he is such a busy man that he will be unable to give me more than half an hour of his time. In fact, he gives me more than twice that; before him is the list of questions that I had been instructed to supply in advance and he works his way steadily through them, supporting each answer with facts and figures. The primátor is direct and unfailingly courteous; indeed, apart from the *slivovice* and the Závodní Stráž, the occasion is almost exactly like an interview I once had with the mayor of San Francisco.

Prague's mayor does not, of course, preside over such a quarrelsome body as his U.S. counterpart. Although the administrative machine in Czechoslovakia is less monolithic than outsiders suppose, the distinctions are, in practice, very fine indeed between the Communist Party itself and the other components of the country's National Front—a coalition of the Communists; four other, much smaller political parties (including the Socialist Party and the People's Party) that are considered as auxiliaries to the dominant party rather than its rivals; and mass organizations such as the Revolutionary Trade Union Movement and the Socialist Youth Union. The Front provides the reassuring appearance of political consensus; any disagreements among Czechoslovak parliamentarians are strictly not for public consumption.

To a large extent the government of the city mirrors that of the nation. The city is divided into 10 administrative and electoral districts, and every five years all citizens aged 18 or over of each district are invited to elect new representatives to the Prague National Committee—chosen, of course, from a list of officially approved candidates nominated by the medley of organizations that makes up the National Front. According to the primátor, problems have sometimes been caused by the rule that at least one-third of the Committee's members should be "workers"; when selecting candidates, he explained, it was often difficult to decide if an individual who already had substantial experience in local government could still be considered a "worker". After such awkwardnesses have been ironed out, there begins a three-month political campaign that culminates in the election of the councillors who will govern Prague; in the late 1970s there were 183 of them, about one for every 7,000 voters.

The curious fictions that typify Czech political life are well demonstrated by the phenomenon of the People's Party. It differs from the Communist Party only insofar as its origins lie in the Roman Catholic Church and not in professed atheism; although the party's religious allegiance is today little more than nominal. It does have its own newspaper, *Lidová demokracie*, which competes for circulation with numerous other publications such as *Rudé právo*, the Communist Party paper; *Práce*, the organ of the trade-union movement; and *Mladá fronta*, which represents the youth organiza-

Near Wenceslas Square, a surveyor employed by the Prague National Committee—the city's administrative council—records the measurements that her colleague is taking with a theodolite. Women make up almost half of the labour force in Czechoslovakia.

tions; but when Pope John Paul II visited his native Poland in 1979, *Lidová demokracie* scarcely mentioned the event.

The city which the primátor and his National Committee govern so exactingly has experienced a curiously uneven pattern of expansion throughout its history. Late in the 14th Century, during the enlightened reign of Charles IV, the population of the Czech capital increased from 15,000 to 40,000, making it, after Rome, the second largest city in Europe. Thereafter, Prague languished for five centuries—although the gradual absorption of its neighbouring villages throughout the 19th Century led to a slow upturn in population. The proclamation of Czechoslovakia's independence in 1918 stimulated a threefold population increase and, by 1938, Prague had one million inhabitants. In the years since then, only 200,000 have been added to that figure.

Prague's slow growth in recent times—which is quite inconsistent with the tendency in so many other world capitals—is partly a result of sombre historical events. The Second World War not only retarded the city's birthrate but also led to the deaths of many Praguers at the hands of the Nazis. In Czechoslovakia as a whole, about 240,000 citizens—roughly one in 60 of the population—lost their lives during the six years of German occupation; 77,000 of them were Jews. Later, during the Communist purges of 1948 to 1956, an estimated 100,000 Czechs were sent to prison camps for political reasons; not all of them survived and many of those who were eventually released did not return to their place of origin. Furthermore, since 1945 the birthrate in Czechoslovakia has remained low. In Prague, it has frequently fallen below the mortality rate. Faced with the city's chronic housing shortage and an unsteady economic climate that often requires both partners to take full-time jobs, many couples have simply abandoned the idea of trying to raise a family. In a span of less than 10 years some 800,000 legal abortions were performed in a country of only 14 million inhabitants.

Official action has also played a part. The primátor told me that the Czech authorities have deliberately set out to discourage migration from the provinces to the metropolis. The nation's resources have been spread as widely as possible in order to make small communities still viable—and less of a source of discontent than they have become elsewhere in the world during the past generations. The policy is not foolproof, but in Prague's case it has produced impressive results. The annual average of newcomers to the capital has been 15,000; at the same time, however, some 10,000 people have moved out each year. Moreover, it has been decided to maintain the trend until the end of this century. By the year 2000, Prague's population is expected to have risen by no more than 150,000; and the city's built-up area, now covering just under 200 square miles, will have grown by perhaps four square miles.

You can, of course, make predictions about population growth and expect them to be approximately accurate only when—like the Communist State—you rigorously control most aspects of human behaviour. At the level of the Prague National Committee, every feature of the city's administration is organized into a succession of Five-Year Plans that are rigidly adhered to once they have been drafted. These are supplemented by a long-term development plan—divided into nine sections covering such topics as transport, education and health care—that sketches out municipal action until the year 2000. The city councillors are split into 15 working commissions, each of which deals with a different aspect of the current Five-Year Plan and, in addition, keeps an eye on long-term strategy.

All this sounds complicated enough, but on top of everything else the hard-pressed councillors are expected to tackle a number of specific problems afflicting Prague. I asked the primátor for an example. "Well," he said, "at present we're trying to decide what kind of tree we should plant in the city that will survive our polluted atmosphere." This is, indeed, a matter for concern in Prague, which is wealthier in vegetation than most of the European cities I know. Wenceslas Square, for example, is thickly lined with trees and they are well cared for. Every few days municipal workmen pull up the huge, cast-iron grid that surrounds the base of each tree, remove the cigarette ends that passers-by have flicked there and stir up the soil in order to ventilate the tree's roots. But with so much coal dust and soot in the air, this attention alone is not enough.

Seized by a sudden impulse to be constructive, I said, "Why don't you get in touch with Kew Gardens in England? They've had a lot of experience with pollution. I mean, if the London plane tree could survive the dreadful

Female municipal workers spend the morning clearing away fallen leaves on Strelecky Island, a popular wooded haven in the middle of the Vltava River.

smogs we used to have, it can survive anything." The primátor did not bat an eyelid—indeed, he seemed not to have heard my outburst at all—so I subsided into my chair. "What happens," I next asked, "when you have solved all your list of problems—what do you do then?" The slightest twinkle of amusement showed in the primátor's eye. "There are *always* the same number of problems to be solved," he said. "As soon as we get rid of one, we look around for another to take its place."

When speaking of the rigorous control exercised by Communist administrations, one does well to avoid assumptions based entirely upon hearsay or upon the accounts of those who may have personal reasons for being prejudiced against the regime. Grim events do take place in Prague today —for example, within the bleak walls of Pankrác Prison, two miles south of the city centre. But such infamies are not ubiquitous, nor even very frequent; there are many positive aspects to life in Prague.

A major case in point is the educational system. One of the city's most prestigious institutions is the Czechoslovak Academy of Sciences, an élitist body that imitates Russian practice by admitting only the finest academic minds and insulating them from the rough-and-tumble of ordinary student life; and elsewhere in Prague, there are a dozen other establishments of university status. Of these, the Charles University is now merely the most senior in age; the largest is the Czech Technical University, with 15,000 students. Responsibility for these institutions rests with the Ministry of Education, which controls the number of student places available and the quotas for each academic discipline; in recent years, the Ministry has set out to encourage scientific and technical studies.

At a lower level there are more than 400 schools offering primary and secondary education; and here one can see how, paradoxically, the rigid philosophy of the Communist Party has submitted to the educational flexibility that Comenius advised 300 years ago. By the age of about nine, a child's distinctive talent is beginning to show itself. At that point, Prague's educational authorities, in consultation with the parents, devise a special curriculum that will give each child progressively wider opportunities to develop that special intellectual or physical strength, while continuing to provide an all-round education. For those pupils who are particularly gifted in one field, there are 33 secondary schools where the majority of the lessons are devoted to the special subject.

One of the most celebrated of these schools is the Prague Conservatory, which has been functioning since 1884 on the Vltava's east bank, a thousand yards below the Charles Bridge. There, 1,200 students between 14 and 18 years of age, from all over Czechoslovakia, attend 21 different faculties catering for all forms of musical expression, as well as for drama and dance. The students have the best teachers the country can provide and the best pupils graduate to the Academy of Dramatic, Film and Musical

Poised to cross the road, a Praguer carries over his shoulder a replacement panel for the front of his car.

A Passion for Cars

Cherished status symbols, automobiles are more plentiful in Czechoslovakia than in most East European countries. The high purchase price—a Czech-built Škoda, for example, costs about twice the average annual wage—ensures that, once acquired, vehicles are maintained with loving care. But the expense and scarcity of spare parts, together with the unreliable service provided by garages, oblige the majority of Praguers to adopt the do-it-yourself approach. In backyards, parking lots and side-streets all over the city, devoted owners tinker with their engines and retouch bodywork in a patient bid to preserve the appearance and prolong the working life of their vehicles.

174/ **Under the Communist Yoke**

In the suburb of Zabehlice, a watchful car-owner curbs an outbreak of corrosion by delicately dabbing at damaged areas with an anti-rust coat of paint.

An amateur mechanic makes minor repairs to his beloved car in a parking lot where vehicles are cosseted against the elements by protective canvas covers.

In a quiet back-street, a motorist retouches the paintwork of his East German-made automobile. The chain on the steering wheel is a deterrent to thieves.

Using a special cradle to gain access to the underside of his Czech-built Skoda, this Praguer has turned the vehicle on its side to make necessary repairs.

Arts, based next door in the House of Artists—an impressive, late-19th-Century building whose concert hall is the normal home of the Czech Philharmonic, the nation's finest orchestra. From the Academy comes a steady stream of reinforcements for the professional musicians of Czechoslovakia; and those students who do not quite make the professional grade simply add to the rich reservoir of informal musical talent that has long been part of the national heritage.

But education in Prague is not without its flaws. Predictably, the teaching is affected by political indoctrination. The teaching profession itself has suffered since 1968, when those members who had associated themselves publicly with the movement for political reform were swiftly purged after "normalization" began. Today, those who teach must exercise discretion; for example, a teacher may not feel free to attend church lest one of his pupils see him there. In theory, religious observance is tolerated in Czechoslovakia; but when practised by someone in a position of responsibility it can be a risky freedom.

Moreover, educational advancement does not always proceed on the basis of merit alone. Preferential treatment is accorded the children of Communist Party members—but only about one in 15 Czechs is "invited" to join the Party. However, a Prague parent who is not a Party member can still get his child into a preferred school or university by approaching someone influential in the city administration, and, better still, by handing over to him a sealed envelope containing banknotes. Another frequent prerequisite is that the child be a keen member of one of the official youth organizations: the Pioneers, for those under 15, and the Socialist Youth Union thereafter. On the other hand, any child of politically "unacceptable" parents who applies for a university place is automatically rejected.

But, significantly, although the reformers of 1968 would have changed much in Czech society that had gone awry during the previous 20 years of Communism, they showed no wish to alter radically what is in many ways an enlightened and successful system of schooling. Even to an outsider wholly unsympathetic to the excesses of the Czech Communist regime, education in Prague does seem to be organized with an unusually careful consideration of the pupil's well-being. For example, any child who lives more than a few blocks away from his school is provided with two sets of textbooks: one set for home use and one for the school desk, so the pupil need not be wearied by carrying a heavy satchel to and fro each day.

The money to finance the city's educational system—and the many other responsibilities of the Prague National Committee—comes from three sources. By far the largest proportion, about 75 per cent, is provided by the national government. Next come the profits from commercial enterprises owned by the National Committee: about 24 per cent. The smallest contribution, rather less than 1 per cent, comes from what the primátor described

On a street corner near Wenceslas Square, an elderly woman sells evening newspapers. In order to alleviate Czechoslovakia's chronic labour shortage, old-age pensioners—who make up one-quarter of Prague's population—are encouraged by the authorities to continue working after the official retirement age.

to me as "fines"; in fact, a category that includes the revenue from fees such as those charged for dog licences, which, at 1,200 crowns (about $130) each, must be the most expensive in the world. When the cost of licences first shot up to this astronomic level, some of Prague's many dog-owners tried to have their family pets re-classified as watchdogs, for which the licence fee was not increased.

Fines—in their generally accepted sense—are, however, levied for all the usual misdemeanours, ranging from illegal parking to contravention of the strict building regulations. In Prague, it is absolutely forbidden to erect any structure more than 30 metres (100 feet) high unless the State ordains it. The last time I was there, I heard about a builder who had calculated incorrectly and put up an apartment block that exceeded the permitted height by a little more than one metre; he was obliged not only to pay a heavy fine but also to remove the top storey of the offending building.

One curious result of Prague's civic monopoly is that the fining of this unfortunate builder represented for the National Committee both income *and* expenditure. The man was not, of course, engaged in private enterprise; there is no such thing in Prague (except perhaps for the small-scale selling by farmers of their surplus flowers and vegetables at the street market on Havelská, in the Old Town). The builder had erected the apartments at the bidding of one of the city's 15 working commissions; and his salary, as well as his gang's, was paid by yet another commission that had employed the work-force to labour at its direction. So the fine simply meant the ladling of money from one set of municipal accounts to another.

The National Committee's many commercial activities include operating the city's fleet of taxis. Prague cabs may appear to belong to a variety of different firms; but they are, in fact, all controlled by competing managerial staffs within the same municipal "firm". Although the national government normally takes charge of all major industrial and agricultural activities, the city itself runs a few small factories, as well as some farms in the neighbouring countryside. In fact, everyone in Prague is employed either by the municipality or by the State. (Even those essentially solitary creatures, the creative artists, do not escape; a Czech concert pianist who performs all over the world is allowed to accept bookings only via Pragokoncert, a state agency that takes a cut of his foreign earnings and pays him a wage for his appearances within Czechoslovakia.)

This tight, centralized control is exercised over a city that became a major industrial centre in the heyday of the Austro-Hungarian Empire and has remained so ever since, in spite of all the vicissitudes of the Czech economy —which was plundered by the Nazis and which, since 1948, has become little more than a colonial appendage to the Soviet economy.

Today, the biggest industrial concern in Prague is Č.K.D. (Českomoravska Kolben Danek), which makes heavy electrical goods such as locomotives, transformers and compressors. Almost as large are Tesla, another electrical engineering firm; the Klement Gottwald Works, which produces trucks, trams and railway wagons; and the Praga automobile factory. Indeed, half of Prague's workers are employed in engineering, and the city accounts for almost one-fifth of Czechoslovakia's total output of machinery.

But there are, in addition, something like a hundred other, more delicate types of manufacturing currently being carried on in Prague, including optics, electronics, printing and clothing. Although most of these activities are controlled by the national government, the Prague National Committee does have some influence on the planning of new local projects; it aims, for example, to have all industry not absolutely vital to Prague sited outside the city, in order to minimize such problems as air pollution.

Prague has a total labour force of almost 700,000 people; nearly half of them are women, because of the pressing need to supplement family income. The National Committee directly employs 155,000—including 28,000 in public transport, 25,000 in health care, 21,000 in education and 12,000 in community services—while the remainder work in industry and in shops and offices.

Each day, an enormous amount of commuting goes on, with 90,000 people coming into Prague from nearby suburbs and 55,000 leaving the

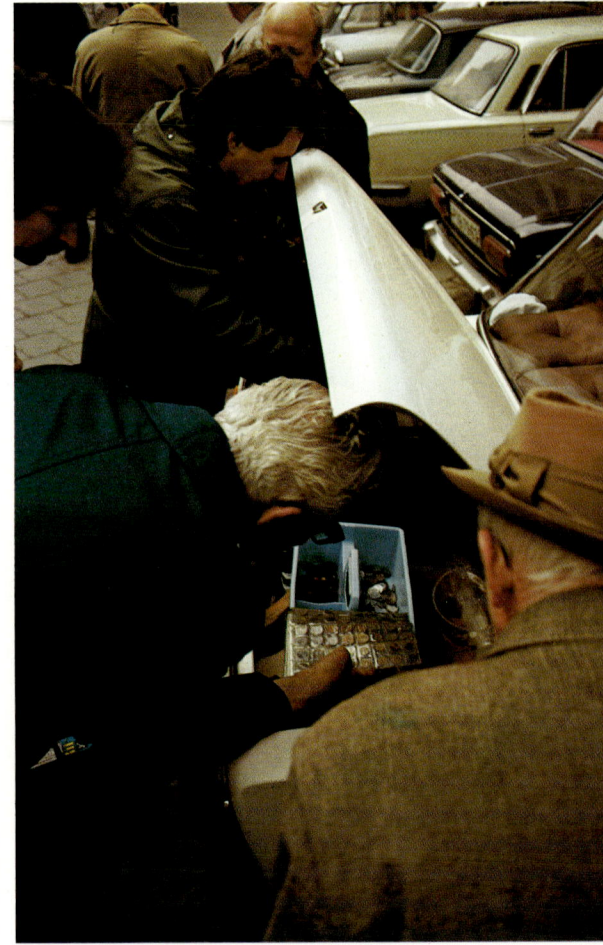

At a market held every Sunday morning in Prague's Old Town district, connoisseurs gather around a selection of old coins on display in the back of a car. The collecting of coins, lapel badges and other small items is a popular Prague hobby, indulged in more for the fun and social contact the activity provides than for financial gain.

city for places of work outside (a large proportion of whom are heading for the coal mines and steelworks of Kladno, 20 miles to the west). Since only about half of the city's 230,000 owners of private cars use their vehicles to travel to work each morning, public transport is one of the National Committee's most vital responsibilities; in fact, it employs almost half as many workers in this capacity as London, a city six times larger. To an outsider, Prague's transport system is certainly impressive.

There are three railway stations to take care of the long-distance commuters and, each morning, more than a million people are brought into Prague from the outer suburbs by bus. But the backbone of Prague's public transport has traditionally been the tramcar and, of the three million passengers who move about within the city every day, at least half still travel in this way. Prague trams are vehicles of great character, with their cream-coloured roofs and their bright red flanks embellished with the city's coat of arms: a clenched fist between two towers, surmounted by the motto *Praha Matka Měst* ("Prague, the Mother of Cities"). Two tramcars are usually coupled together, so that the driver—who can be of either sex—has to keep a sharp eye open for passengers who may have got stuck in the folding doors of the hindmost car.

Like the double-decker buses of London and the cable cars of San Francisco, the trams of Prague are inseparable from the city's image. They are constantly squeezing their way through the narrow streets of Malá Strana and bowling across the bridges spanning the Vltava, or pouring down the slope of Wenceslas Square and at the bottom lurching right into Na příkopé or left into Národní třída. Eventually, they plod uphill towards their ultimate destination in the outlying suburbs, where they are obliged to share the road with mere buses.

I do not think I have ever waited more than 10 minutes for a tramcar in Prague. They are also inexpensive to ride; the Prague National Committee subsidizes such an essential service, so that you can travel any distance for just one crown (about 10 cents). You buy the tickets in batches beforehand—at news-stands, transport offices or hotels—and punch them yourself as you climb aboard. Newcomers to Prague are apt to emerge from their first few tram rides with the strong suspicion that they are the only passengers doing any punching and that the locals either do not have tickets or are saving them for another day. In fact, most Praguers travel on season tickets or on special passes awarded free of charge or at a reduced rate to war veterans, the disabled and other deserving groups.

One day, sad to say, the trams will vanish from Prague—although I am convinced that the only citizens who will genuinely rejoice at their disappearance are those impatient motorists who cannot bear to give way to them in the city's narrow streets—for the National Committee, like municipal authorities almost everywhere, has surrendered to the lure of Progress; in this case, an overwhelming enthusiasm for shifting people from point A to point B underground. One of the long-term strategies that the councillors are implementing is the gradual replacement of the city's tram system by the Prague Metro, which is already an established concern.

When I first came to Prague in 1968, the sole manifestation of the Metro was a great deal of digging in the city centre, accompanied by clouds of dust. The excavations at each end of Wenceslas Square were fenced off with corrugated-iron barricades, in the lee of which, on Sunday mornings, citizens would take shelter from the dust while engaging in a popular local hobby, the buying, selling or swapping of small enamelled lapel badges bearing designs that range from Lenin's face to the symbol of Montreal's Expo 67 or Manchester's Belle Vue Speedway.

Today, the badge-sellers have moved elsewhere and the barricades have disappeared; in their place are two new Metro stations that are models of their kind. Their broad underground concourses are lined with shops and embellished with examples of modern sculpture and decorative mosaics; most importantly, they are spacious enough to allow Praguers to flow towards the escalators at the end of the working day without having to behave like stampeding cattle.

Prague's other Metro stations are equally attractive. At the Malostranska Station you rise straight out of the ground into a garden where people lounge in the sun beside ornamental pools, overlooked on one side by the walls of the Waldstein Palace and on the other by the steep, cobbled route up to Prague Castle. (At Gottwald Station, just south of the New Town, an otherwise excellent view is rather spoiled by the sight of Pankrác Prison.) Down below, where the platforms are, each station is painted a different colour—such as green, dark red or gold—that is remarkably soothing. The trains themselves are roomy and comfortable and at each stop a tape-recorded female voice announces the name of the station, followed a few seconds later by a chime of bells warning that the doors are about to close. Not surprisingly, when the initial stretch of the Metro was opened in 1973 and the National Committee announced in celebration that all travel on the first day would be free, Czechs and Slovaks poured into Prague from all over the country to share in this new piece of fun.

By the end of the 1970s, Prague had almost 10 miles of Metro in operation. As on the trams, you can travel as far as you like for one crown. The planners hope that, by the year 2000, the system will have expanded to almost 50 miles, serving a hundred stations.

By then, perhaps, Praguers will have forgotten their solitary grumble about the new system. The gigantic Č.K.D. works on the outskirts of the city could have manufactured perfectly good trains for the Metro. Instead, because of the economic imperialism that prevails in Eastern Europe, the National Committee was obliged to buy them from the Soviet Union. There is nothing at all wrong with these Russian-built underground trains—but Praguers reckon that that is rather beside the point.

In the city's New Town district, art nouveau décor graces the interior of the Zivnostenska Bank, a major dealer in foreign currency from both capitalist and Communist countries. The bank sells foreign denominations to those Praguers who are allowed to travel outside Czechoslovakia, and purchases currency from citizens who have received remittances from relatives living or working abroad.

Anyone accustomed to riding the underground systems of Western Europe is struck by the complete absence of commercial advertising on the Prague Metro. In fact, few billboards deface the city. In some streets, on the barriers erected to shield passers-by from the mess of building construction or restoration, you may see a few dozen posters advertising such events as art exhibitions, concerts or moto-cross rallies—but that is all. And because there is no private enterprise in Prague you will look in vain for a shop that displays the name of an owner, or even an individual trade-name; the shops merely bear a description of what they sell, such as *potraviny* (food), *lékárna* (pharmacy) or *cukrárna* (confectioner's). The only place where I have ever noticed neon signs at night is Wenceslas Square, and even those mostly draw attention to Centrotex, Pragoexport and other, similarly inscrutable trading corporations of the Communist bloc; if you look hard, however, you can occasionally catch a glimpse of such solid capitalist names as Fiat and Olivetti too.

During a visit to Prague in 1979, by far the largest hoarding I saw extended for a good 50 yards along Na příkopé. It bore the photographs of 80 people, all of whom looked utterly worthy and even rather stern. I was told that they were the Exemplary Workers, chosen each year by the various trade unions. They are the men and women who never clock in a minute late at the factory, never take a day off "to go to Granny's funeral" and who always exceed the individual productivity targets that are set by the municipality or by the State.

The Na příkopé display—together with comparable ones elsewhere in the city that extol the virtues of Communism or of friendship with the Soviet Union—was just one manifestation of the non-stop onslaught of propaganda to which the ordinary Praguer is subjected. Each item of television news appears to be chosen as much for its propaganda value as for its journalistic content; for example, a film of the Queen of England, dressed in tiara and gorgeous robes, driving off to open a new session of Parliament might be juxtaposed with one showing British miners demonstrating outside a pit. Similarly, the front pages of all Prague's six daily newspapers contain more or less the same pre-selected items of daily news (or non-news); only the layout is different.

There are, also, places called "Agitation Centres", where you can obtain Communist literature, posters and flags. They also have maps showing how the Soviet armies of liberation swept across Czechoslovakia from the east in 1945. Rather than publicize the U.S. Army's contribution, the western side of such maps is left blank.

Such official propaganda is ultimately self-defeating; most Praguers have ready access to information from the West—either by listening to Radio Free Europe (broadcast from Munich, less than 200 miles away), to the BBC and Vienna Radio, or via friends and relatives abroad—and they bitterly resent local distortions of the facts. Even when the official news media report the truth, they are often not believed. As an instance, a story about a temporary, but quite genuine, sugar shortage in Britain was widely dismissed as a fabrication. And all this takes place in a country where *Pravda Vítězí* ("Truth Shall Prevail") has been a slogan proudly used by national heroes from Hus to Masaryk!

Nonetheless, Prague in some respects still compares favourably with the cities of the West. No one who values comfort, efficiency and personal safety could sensibly claim that he would rather ride the New York subway than the Prague Metro. And most Western mayors would give their eye-teeth to be able to exchange their own city's crime rate for that of Prague. (I use the word "crime" in the generally accepted sense; I am not referring to the odious process whereby Praguers end up in Pankrác merely for having dissented from the State's views.)

To begin with the less serious misdemeanours, you hardly ever see a drunk in the streets of Prague—even though the Czechs are among the world's champion drinkers. They have learnt to practise this pursuit only in private, since the official treatment accorded those found drunk in public is brisk: the offender is hustled into police custody overnight, placed in a special sobering-up clinic and, on his release next morning, presented with a stiff bill for both accommodation and the attention required to restore him to sobriety. The penalties for drunken driving are, not surprisingly, considerably more severe. Even so, the Prague authorities claim that an estimated 45 per cent of all criminal offences are committed under the influence of alcohol.

Juvenile crime remains at a remarkably low level for a city of 1.2 million people; in one recent year, only 329 offenders under the age of 18 appeared before the Prague courts. One reason for this may be that, under Czech law, no child under 15 can be punished for breaking the law—although the parents are, if their offspring is found guilty.

Major crimes seem equally uncommon: in that same year, 13 people were found guilty of murder and sentenced to up to 15 years' imprisonment (the death penalty is still on the statute book, but is exacted only in cases of exceptionally brutal killings); 28 convicted rapists were given between three and 12 years; and 83 persons found guilty of robbery with violence faced prison terms of up to 10 years.

One category of crime peculiar to the Czech way of life can be roughly translated as "robbing socialist society"; officially it accounts for 20 per cent of all offences committed in Prague. There is even a special Department of Economic Criminality, for whose powers of investigation the Czechs have a healthy respect. Some years ago, a Prague acquaintance of mine sold a car, quite legally, to someone he knew only as a prospective buyer. Months later, my friend was suddenly summoned to attend the Department and spent the intervening couple of days anxiously wondering what on earth he

In the pleasantly furnished sitting room of their private house, a Prague couple entertain a guest over coffee. Such space and comfort is by no means typical of accommodation in the overcrowded city: only a privileged minority of citizens—including Party officials, senior civil servants and prominent scientists, artists and athletes—can afford to buy their own homes; the majority live in rented municipal apartments.

was going to be accused of. It turned out that he had done nothing wrong and the authorities duly conceded the fact; the man who had bought his car had been arrested for selling automobile spare parts on the black market, and so the Department had methodically set out to question everyone with whom the accused was known to have been in contact for some considerable time past.

Aside from black marketeering, "robbing socialist society" can include taking home from the office a couple of ball-point pens or using an official car to take your girl friend for a spin in the country—as well as such misdemeanours as strawberry pilfering. The culprits who were pilloried in the Czech Press some years ago were workers on one of the National Committee's farms just outside the city boundary. It was their job to gather fruit destined for the street market on Havelská, also operated by the Committee. Unwisely, the pickers attempted a spot of private enterprise by selling the strawberries directly to customers instead of sending them to market.

Prague's enviably low incidence of serious crime cannot entirely be the consequence of the city's large police force (abetted by a widespread network of informers), together with courts that can hand out quite harsh

At the Mánes Art Gallery in the New Town district, three youngsters scrutinize a striking canvas hung for a special children's exhibition. Named after Josef Mánes, a 19th-Century artist revered as the founder of modern Czech painting, the gallery is funded by the Ministry of Culture and presents frequently changing exhibitions of contemporary art.

sentences; the official campaign to instil into Praguers a sense of civic responsibility also plays a constructive part. The trouble is, a regime that sets out to suppress irresponsibility also tends to suppress other spontaneous human impulses. As long ago as 1924, in his essay "Why I am not a Communist", the famous Czech playwright Karel Čapek made a remark that is still strikingly relevant to the predicament of Prague: "The language of Communism is hard, it is not sentimental... only a cad and a demagogue are not sentimental. Without sentimental reasons, you would not pass a glass of water to another human being."

It is this rejection of the sentimental (by which I mean the opposite of unfeeling rigidity) that lies at the bottom of so much that is hard to bear in Prague nowadays. As an example, it is responsible for the menacing questions that must be answered by everyone seeking employment in the city; there is a standard form to be filled in that inquires into the political affiliations of the applicant's family and the applicant's own "political posture during the critical period 1968-69".

The State tends to be equally heavy-handed whenever it seeks to wave the flag, to promote patriotism, in an organized way. And it is consistently at its worst during that great annual socialist festival, May Day. Then, as many foreign observers have noted, most of Prague seems to turn out to watch the huge parade of workers and young people that is held at Letná, just north of the Old Town. In fact, most Praguers feel obliged to turn out. (Just as, on this and other days of official celebration, they feel obliged to display both the Czech and the Soviet flags in the windows of their homes; if both flags are not on display, someone comes round to find out why not. And woe betide the Praguer who hangs out the Czech flag alone; that is considered a provocative gesture.

Weeks before May Day, notices listing arrangements for the holiday are posted in factories, shops and offices, usually accompanied by sheets of blank paper ruled into three columns. Those who wish to take part in the parade itself are invited to sign their names in the first column. Those who wish only to watch are asked to sign in the second—in which case they must gather at a pre-arranged point, where someone from the works will come along and check to see that all the signatories are, in fact, present. The third column is reserved for those who wish neither to march nor to watch. It usually remains blank.

The last time I was in Prague coincided with the celebration of Liberation Day on May 9, the anniversary of the arrival in the city of Soviet troops in 1945. Shop windows all over the city displayed the same poster: a photograph taken in 1945 of a Red Army soldier sitting on his tank with a small Czech boy on his knee, the soldier looking protective and strong, the child smiling happily at him.

In the evening, the newspapers had announced, there was to be a celebratory fireworks display from Strahov Hill. As far as I know, no one was asked to inform his boss as to whether or not he meant to attend; but, in fact, so many people crowded on to the east bank of the Vltava in order to get the best view of the fireworks that traffic was brought to a standstill half an hour before proceedings began. The display was a marvellous spectacle: for 30 minutes without a break rockets and star-shells shot into the night sky above Prague, drenching the castle with vivid light that changed colour each time a fresh volley was unloosed.

It was the kind of magical excitement that normally incites young children to jump up and down and shout with delight. But the strange thing was that all those thousands of people, and all those children perched on adult shoulders, watched without a sound.

In Celebration of May Day

Czech and Soviet flags decorate a house window for May Day. Correctly oriented to the occupants' view, the emblems are reversed to the outside world.

For some 250,000 Praguers, the public holiday of May 1 means actively marching in the May Day parade. Another 150,000 or so turn out to watch the event, first held in 1890 as an expression of Czech nationalism and now—as in other Communist states—a highly organized celebration of working-class solidarity. Traditionally staged in Wenceslas Square, the procession's venue was moved in the 1970s to Letná Plain, a spacious open field on a hilltop north of the city centre that was cleared of old houses and levelled in the 1950s. Grouped by factory, school or district, the marchers assemble at 9 a.m. for a speech by the nation's President, then parade past the grandstand that holds high-ranking government and Party officials. By 1 p.m., their duties discharged, participants and spectators can spend the rest of the holiday as they wish.

Following a tradition begun in the 1930s, women workers and housewives from Žižkov, one of the city's oldest industrial areas, lead off the parade in white.

A distinguished, bemedalled old soldier views the march from a place of honour on one of the grandstands.

In front of a giant portrait of the Czech President, a gaily dressed child greets the procession with a paper flower and a Soviet flag provided by her school.

Officers of the army and of the volunteer People's Militia guard the grandstand where members of the country's ruling élite review the parade from on high.

Among placards including a dove of peace, a fervent spectator clenches fists in a gesture of solidarity.

A smiling member of the Socialist Youth Union carries the movement's flag.

Wearing a red May Day headscarf, a marcher advances with her contingent.

Spectators joining the main procession flourish their handkerchiefs and paper streamers in the direction of the dignitaries on the principal grandstand.

After the parade, a member of the People's Militia pauses on a park bench before leaving Letná Plain. The furled trade-union flag belongs to the factory where he works. Soon after the procession is over, traffic starts to move again and, within a few hours, a small army of street cleaners has swept away all traces of the parade.

Bibliography

Bartoš, František, *Bedřich Smetana: Letters and Reminiscences.* Artia, Prague, 1955.
Blažíček, Oldřich J., *Baroque Art in Bohemia.* Hamlyn, London, 1968.
Blom, Eric, *Mozart.* J. M. Dent & Sons, Ltd., London, 1962.
Bradley, J. F. N., *Czechoslovakia.* Edinburgh University Press, 1971.
Brock, Peter, and Gordon Skilling, H. (eds.), *The Czech Renascence of the Nineteenth Century.* University of Toronto Press, 1970.
Brod, Max, *Biography of Franz Kafka.* Secker & Warburg, Ltd., London, 1948.
Burian, Jiří, and Hartmann, Antonín, *Prague Castle.* Hamlyn, London, 1975.
Burke, John, *Czechoslovakia.* B. T. Batsford, Ltd., London, 1976.
Eisner, Pavel, *Franz Kafka and Prague.* Golden Griffin Books, New York, 1950.
Hašek, Jaroslav, *The Good Soldier Švejk* (trans. Cecil Parrott). Heinemann, Ltd., London, 1973.
Hermann, A. H., *A History of the Czechs.* Allen Lane, London, 1975.
Knox, Brian, *The Architecture of Prague and Bohemia.* Faber & Faber Ltd., London, 1962.
Korbel, Josef, *Twentieth-Century Czechoslovakia: The Meanings of its History.* Columbia University Press, New York, 1977.
Korecký, Miroslav, *Prague in Colour.* Hamlyn, London, 1975.
Krejčí, Jaroslav, *Social Change and Stratification in Postwar Czechoslovakia.* Macmillan Press, Ltd., London, 1972.
Kusin, Vladimir V., *From Dubček to Charter 77.* Q Press Ltd., Edinburgh, 1978.
Landisch, Bohumil, *Praha.* Olympia, Prague, 1968.
Lutzow, Franz Count, *The Story of Prague.* J. M. Dent & Sons, Ltd., London, 1907.
Lutzow, Franz Count, *Bohemia: An Historical Sketch.* J. M. Dent & Sons, Ltd., London, 1939.
Mann, Golo, *Wallenstein* (trans. C. Kessler). André Deutsch, Ltd., London, 1976.
Mucha, Jiří (ed.), *The Graphic Work of Alphonse Mucha.* Academy Editions, London, 1973.
Nagel Publishers, *Encyclopedia-Guide: Czechoslovakia.* Geneva, 1975.
Newmarch, Rosa, *The Music of Czechoslovakia.* Oxford University Press, 1942.
Olivova, Vera, *The Doomed Democracy.* Sidgwick & Jackson, Ltd., London, 1972.
Parrott, Cecil, *The Serpent and the Nightingale.* Faber & Faber Ltd., London, 1977.
Parrott, Cecil, *The Bad Bohemian: A Life of Jaroslav Hašek.* The Bodley Head, Ltd., London, 1978.
Pech, Stanley, *The Czech Revolution of 1848.* The University of North Carolina Press, Chapel Hill, 1969.
Rechcigl Jr., Miloslav (ed.), *Czechoslovakia Past and Present.* Mouton, Paris, 1968.
Robertson, Alec, *Dvořák.* J. M. Dent & Sons, Ltd., London, 1974.
Roth, Ernst, *A Tale of Two Cities.* Cassell & Co., Ltd., London, 1971.
Rybár, Ctibor, *Prague.* Olympia, Prague, 1973.
Schwartz, Harry, *Prague's 200 Days.* Pall Mall Press Ltd., London, 1969.
Shawcross, William, *Dubček.* Weidenfeld & Nicolson Ltd., London, 1970.
Šourek, Otakar, *Antonín Dvořák: His Life and Works.* Orbis, Prague, 1952.
Spinka, Matthew, *John Hus, A Biography.* Princeton University Press, 1968.
Svoboda, Alois, *Prague, An Intimate Guide.* Sportovni a Turisticke Nakladatelstvi, Prague, 1965.
Táborský, Edward, *Communism in Czechoslovakia 1948-1960.* Princeton University Press, 1961.
Tigrid, Pavel, *Why Dubček Fell.* Macdonald & Co., Ltd., London, 1971.
Ulč, Otto, *Politics in Czechoslovakia.* W. H. Freeman & Co., Ltd., 1974.
Wallace, William V., *Czechoslovakia.* Ernest Benn, Ltd., London, 1976.
Zeman, Zbyněk, *Prague Spring.* Penguin Books Limited, Harmondsworth, Middlesex, 1969.
Zeman, Zbyněk, *The Masaryks.* Weidenfeld & Nicolson Ltd., London, 1976.

Acknowledgements and Picture Credits

The editors wish to thank the following for their valuable assistance: Mike Brown, London; Richard Carlisle, Great Bookham, Surrey; Dagmar Hogan, Manchester; Jeremy Lawrence, London; Maria McLoughlin, Feltham, Middlesex; Frances Middlestorb, Sheffield; Winona O'Connor, London; Palach Press Ltd., London; Jitka Paterson, Frating near Colchester, Essex; Hans Tasiemka Archive, London; Giles Wordsworth, London.

Sources for all pictures in this book are shown below. Credits for the pictures from left to right are separated by commas, from top to bottom by dashes.

All photographs are by Kees van den Berg except: pages 6, 9—Patrick Ward, London. 14, 15—Map by Hunting Surveys Ltd., London (Silhouettes by Norman Bancroft-Hunt, Caterham Hill, Surrey). 19—Süddeutscher Verlag, Munich. 21—Novosti Press Agency, London. 22—Camera Press Ltd., London. 24—Marilyn Silverstone/Magnum from the John Hillelson Agency, London. 25—Magnum from the John Hillelson Agency—Jevan Berrange/RBO Camera Press Ltd. 53, 55, 62-66, 74, 75—Patrick Ward. 76—Mary Evans Picture Library, London. 80, 81—Czechoslovak News Agency, Prague. 84, 85, 92—Patrick Ward. 94—Banknote designed by Alphonse Mucha; Stanley Gibbons Currency Ltd., London, by courtesy of Jiří Mucha, Prague; photo: Rodney Todd-White & Son, London. 95—Alphonse Mucha 1912 Lottery Poster by courtesy of Jiří Mucha © by S.P.A.D.E.M. Paris 1980, Lords Gallery, London; photo: David Brinson, London. 96—Alphonse Mucha 1928 Slav Epic Poster by courtesy of Jiří Mucha © S.P.A.D.E.M. Paris 1980, Lords Gallery; photo: David Brinson. 98—Oskar Kokoschka "Thomas G. Masaryk" © by A.D.A.G.P. Paris 1980, Museum of Art, Carnegie Institute, Pittsburgh, Pennsylvania; photo: Elton Schnellbacher, Pittsburgh. 100—From "VII Sletu Všesokolskeho Vpraze 1920", School of Slavonic and East European Studies, London. 102, 107—Patrick Ward. 118, 119—Nathan Benn/Woodfin Camp & Associates, New York. 141—(inset) Popperfoto, London. 146—Ullstein, Berlin. 150, 151—(left top, right bottom) by courtesy of Josef Vyletal, Prague; (left bottom, right top) by courtesy of Jiří Salamoun, Prague. 170, 171, 184—Patrick Ward.

Index

Numerals in italics indicate a photograph or drawing of the subject mentioned.

A
Academy of Sciences, Czechoslovak, 16-17, 172
Agriculture, 18, 80, 100
Architects: Aichbauer, Jan Jiří, 126; Dientzenhofer, Christoph and Kilian Ignaz, 111, 116, 125, 130, 131; Matthew of Arras, 55, 81, 82; Pánek, Jan, 128; Parler, Peter, 81, 106
Architecture: art nouveau, *103, 120, 180*; baroque, 8, 14, 84, 91, *106, 108, 108,* 111, 116, 125, *129,* 133; Charles IV's patronage, 14; Gothic, 14, 55, 82, 106, 116; Habsburg influence, 91, 111, *124-31*; neoclassical, 53; 19th-Century, *121*; preservation of heritage, 121-3; Renaissance, *8,* 116; 20th-Century, 120-1, 122
Art galleries: Mánes, 184; National, 104
Artists: Kokoschka, Oskar, 98; Lada, Josef, *144, 150*; Mánes, Josef, 184; Mucha, Alphonse, *94-6*; Nosecký, Father Siard, 108, *108-9*; Svoboda, Josef, 155
Arts and crafts: 91; art nouveau, *46-7, 94, 103, 167, 180*; Bohemian glass, *First end paper*; graphic design, *94-6, 150-1,* 155; painting, 108; plasterwork, *Last end paper*; Rudolf II's patronage, 83, 90, 104; sculpture, *103, 106*; *see also* House-signs, Statues
Austro-Hungarian Empire: 92-3, 97; attitude of Czechs towards, 148, 150; disintegration of, 83, 93, 99; *see also* Habsburg dynasty

B
Beer, 41, 51-3
Beer parlours, *34-5, 41, 47, 49, 52-3,* 109, 116, 144
Beneš, Edvard, Foreign Minister and President, 13, 18, 83, 97, 167
Bohemia and Moravia: 5, 6, 7, 14, 88; decline, 88, 91; early settlers, 6, 14; Estates, 80, 86, 88, 90-1, 92, 104, 108, 109; German inhabitants, 7, 80, 82, 93; under Habsburg rule, 8, 77, 90-1, 92, 93, 104; nobility, 77, 80, 86, 88, 90-1, 92, 104, 108, 109; origin of name, 6; under Přemyslid rule, 7, 82; *see also* Czechoslovakia, Slovakia
Bribery and corruption, 44-5, 176, 183
Britain, and Munich agreement, 10-11
Building and construction: 57, 167; heating systems, *167;* preservation, 121-3; regulations and contravention of, 122, 177-8

C
Cafés, restaurants and clubs, 20, 42, 47, *48, 49, 50-51,* 51, 53, *53,* 61; *see also* Municipal House
Catholic Church, Roman: building, 83; Counter-Reformation, 82, 92; Czech attitude to, 7, 82, 86; and Czech language, 134; forcible conversion to, 91, 125; "Golden Bull", 80; missionaries, 6, 82; murder of Catholics, 87, 88; papacy, 7, 78, 83, 86; People's Party, 168; versus Protestants, 77, 82, 88, 90
Čechy, 6, 82
Chamberlain, Neville, 10-11
Charles IV, King: 7, 78, 80-2, 106; building programme, 14, 80; founding of university, 7, 80-1; "Golden Bull", 80; as law codifier, 80; prosperity and achievement under, 7, 169
Charles Bridge, 14, 77-8, 81, 82, *84-5,* 90, 92
Charles University, 7, 80-1, 82, 86, 92, 172
Charter of 1977, 58, 60-1, 83
Chronology, 82-3
Churches and cathedrals: 111; Basilica of St. George, 104-6; Bethlehem Chapel, 83, 86; Loreto, *126;* Our Lady of Týn, 29, 82, 116, 123; St. Cyril and St. Methodius, 8; St. James, *128, 129,* 133; St. John on the Rock, 111; St. Katherine, 111; St. Lawrence, *110-11;* St. Nicholas (Malá Strana), 108, *130, 131;* St. Nicholas (Staré Město), 6, 111, 116, *124-5;* St. Vitus, *Cover,* 5, 14, *78,* 81, 82, 103. *104-5,* 106
Cinema: Laterna Magica, *148,* 154; "New Wave" films, 154; posters, *150-1*
Comenius (Komenský, Jan), 91-2, *98,* 99, 172
Communism: 17, 18; de-Stalinization, 22; liberalization, 17, 18, 20, 41, 152; normalization, 28, 57, 60
Communist Party of Czechoslovakia: 13, 18, 21, 22, 28, 83, 104, 167; absentees abroad pay compensation, 60; Agitation Centres, 181; criticized in Charter of 1977, 58, 60-1; dissidents and exiles, 60; experiment in social democracy, 8, 11, 17, 18, 20, 41; free speech and movement, 18, 60, 152; nationalization of church property, 111; preferential treatment for members, 176; propaganda, 115, 181-2; purges and executions, 13, 18, 83, 169; small communities encouraged, 170; submission to Moscow (1968), 13, 24, 176
Crime, 182-4
Culture, Ministry of, 135, 148, 184
Currency and finance: 44, 45, 80, 123, 180; Tuzex coupons, 45-6
Czech Army: 26, 28, *192-3;* Czechoslovak Legion, 98; People's Militia, *192-3, 196-7*
Czech nationalism: 7, 81, 93, 97-9, 100, 119, 187; Committee Abroad, 97, 98, 99; and cultural life, 133-4; manifesto of July 1968, 21-3; and Reformation, 82, 88; revival, 83, 134, 140; Slavs versus alien domination, 7, 8, 83, 93, 97, 148; *see also* Hus, Jan, Hussite movement, Language, Sokol movement
Czechoslovakia: 5, 8, 14, 93, 97-9, 169; area and population, 83, 170; frontiers, 5, 44, 99; migration, 170; minorities, 100-1; national anthem, 136; National Assembly, 104; under Nazi rule, 8, 11, 18, 21, 83, 100, 151, 169; under Soviet domination, 8, 13, 24, 26, 28-9; as subject nation, 5-6, 41; *see also* Bohemia and Moravia, Slovakia

D
Daladier, Edouard, 11
Defenestrations, 77, 82, 83, 87, 88, 90
Districts: Josefov, 103, 119-20; Malá Strana (Lesser Quarter), 5, *12-13,* 14, 81, 82, 108; Nové Město (New Town), 14, 81, 82, 111, 120; Staré Město (Old Town), 5, 7, 14, 42, 82, 111, 120, 146, 178
Dubček, Alexander, President: 11, 13, 17-18, 20-2, 24, 26, 28, 83; and "socialism with a human face", 11, 41
Dvořák, Antonín, 134, 141, *142,* 145-8

E
Economy: 46, 80, 82, 99; distorted by Soviet policy, 16, 18, 180; low productivity, 44; private enterprise, 18, 177, 180, 183; small-scale businesses, 100; *see also* Agriculture, Currency and finance, Industry, Trade
Education: 83, 92, 101, 157, 165, 172, 176, 178; compulsory German, 95; Jesuit influence, 91; *see also* Comenius, Language, Universities

F
Ferdinand I, King, 82, 88
Ferdinand II, King, 90
Folk dance, 140-1, 152
Food and drink: *36,* 51, 80, 168; delicacies, *42-3,* 51; *see also* Beer, Beer parlours, Cafés, restaurants and clubs, Hotels, Street markets
Franz Josef, Emperor of Austria, 93
Frederick, Elector Palatine, 90

G
George of Poděbrady, King, 82, 88, 106
German occupation: 8, 10-11, 18, 21, 83, 100, 101, 116, 151, 169; claims on Sudetenland, 10-11
Germans and Germanization: 7, 80, 82, 83, 91, 93, 95, 134, 145, 151; anti-Semitism, 119, 151; at Charles University, 81; Smetana (quoted), 142; support for Rome, 82-3; *see also* Nazis and Nazism
Golden Lane, *91,* 106
Gottwald, Klement, President, 11, 13, 167
Gymnastics, 54, 93, *156-65; see also* Sokol movement

H
Habsburg dynasty, 8, 14, 82, 88, 90, 92, 99, 109
Hašek, Jaroslav, 134, 144, 148, 150
Helsinki agreement, 58, 60, 83
Hitler, Adolf, 10, *18,* 101, 103; *see also* Nazis and Nazism
Holy Roman Empire and Emperors: 7, 78, 80, 82, 83, 86, 88; imperial crusades, 87, 88, 90
Hotels, *First end paper, 46-7,* 51
House-signs, 111, *112-13,* 116
Housing: 45, 101, 170, *183;* modern, 121, *122-3;* as privilege, 57; regulations, 57; tenement, *121,* 135; weekend homes, 56-7, 61, 63, *64, 72-3*
Hradčany (Castle Hill), 5, 6, 14, 81, 82, 103-8, *Last end paper*
Hungary, 6, 7, 28, 82
Hus, Jan: 7, 82, 86, 83, 86, 92, 182; and language reform, 83, 134; memorial, 99, 116
Husák, Gustáv, President, 58, 83
Hussite movement: 82, 86-8, 99; Taborites, 82, 87-8; Wars, 55, 82, 87-8, 111

I
Industry: 14, 16, 92, 100, 178; automobile, 41, 100, 104; heavy engineering, 178; mining, 35, 80, 122, 167

J
Jagiełło dynasty, 82, 88, 104
Jews and Jewish communities: 82, 116, 119-20; anti-Semitism, 119, 151; cemeteries, 51, *117,* 119, 120, 151; concentration camp victims, 120, 169; Town Hall and clock, 119; *see also* Synagogues
John of Luxembourg, King, 7, 78, 82, 133
Josef II, Emperor of Austria, 83, 92-3, 141

K
Kafka, Franz, 134, *146,* 148, 150-2
Karlštejn Castle, 55-6
Kohout, Pavel (quoted), 22-3
Komenský, Jan, *see* Comenius

L
Labour and employment: 31, 42, 170, 178, 184-5; abroad, 46; average wage, 17, 44, 57; exemplary workers, 181; "moonlighting", 44; pensioners, *37, 177;* shortage of workers, 44, 57, 123, 177; women, 31, 42, 44, *169,* 170, *171,* 178, *188-9*
Language: 6, 82, 83; official status for German, 91, 96, 145; reform of Czech, 83, 134; revival, 93; vernacular Bible, 83, 134; *see also* Germans and Germanization
Leopold II, King, 141
Liberation Day, *21,* 26, 185; *see also* Soviet Army
Lidice massacre, 8, 10, 83
Lipany, Battle of, 82, 88
Literature: *135;* epic poem forgeries, 97; freedom of expression, 18, 60, 152; journals, 20, 21-3, 28, 60, 150; museum, 108; vernacular Bible, 83, 134; *see also* Language, Writers, playwrights and poets, Writers' Union *and under individual authors*
Löw, Rabbi, 120, 154
Luxembourg dynasty, 7, 78, 82, 133

M
Map, 14-15
Masaryk: Jan, Foreign Minister, 87; Tomáš Garrigue, President, 97-101, *98*, 182
May Day, *Cover,* 116, 184-5, *186-97*
Mělnik, 77, 80
Moravia, *see* Bohemia and Moravia, Czechoslovakia
Motor vehicles: 41-2, 45, 103, *173-5*, 179; Škoda, 41, 100, 173, *175*
Mozart, Wolfgang Amadeus: 83, 136, 138-9, 141; "Prague" Symphony, 138
Mucha, Alphonse, *94-6*
Munich agreement, 10-11, 83
Municipal House, *50-1*, 120, 135, *136-7*, *139*
Museums: Jewish, 116, 119; Klement Gottwald, 11; Memorial of National Literature, 108; Municipal, 116; National, 6; Smetana, 145; War, *Last end paper*
Music: 133-48, 172, 176; Austrian State Prize, 146, 147; church, 133, 134; Czech Opera, 142, 146; Czech Philharmonic Orchestra, 176; folk, *133*, 134, 141; Hlahol Choral Society, 142; Hussite, 87, 134; jazz, 53; pop, 154-5; state control, 134-5, 155, 178; *see also* Musicians and composers, "Prague Spring" Festival *and under individual names*
Musicians and composers: Benda, František, 134; Brixi, František, 133, 138; Burney, Dr. Charles (quoted), 136; Černohorsky, Friar Bohuslav, 133; Dušek, Josefa and František, 138, 139, 141; Janáček, Leoš, 141; Martinů, Bohuslav, 141; Mysliveček, Josef, 134, 138; Stamic, Jan, 134, 136, 138; *see also under individual names*

N
Nazis and Nazism: fugitives from, 101; Lidice massacre, 8, 10, 83; occupation, 8, 18, 21, 83, 100, 151, 169; vandalism, 115, 116
Nepomuk, St. John of, *92*, *92*, 144
Newspapers: 18, 20, 58, 60, 168-9, 181; *Literární listy,* 20, 21-3, 28, 60
Novotný, Antonín, President, 11, 13, 16-18

O
Old Town Hall: *6*, 116; clock, *10*, *86*, *114*, 115, 116-17
Otakar I, King, 82
Ottoman Empire, 88, 109

P
Palaces: 17, 108, 116; Royal, 104; Schwarzenberg, *Last end paper;* Waldstein (Wallenstein), 109, 111
Palach, Jan, 28-9
Pankrác Prison, 172, 180, 182
Parks, 54, *152*, 154-5
Parrott, Sir Cecil (quoted), 11
Peasantry, 7, 87, 88, 91, 92-3, 97, 134
Petřín Hill, 81, *110-11*
Plzeň, 13, 34
Police: 33, 57, 182-3; Austrian, 88, 93
Political parties: 167; National Front, 168; People's Party, 168; Realists, 97; Young Czechs, 93
Prague: alien domination, 8, 83, 97; architectural heritage, 8, 121-3; area, 5, 170; building regulations, 122; as capital, 5, 150; "City of a Hundred Spires", *6*; city, woodcut of, *80-1*; climate, 54; coat of arms, 179; cultural life, 133-4; in decline, 169; distance from sea, 55; foreign tourists in, 117; foundation and early history, 5, 6, 7, 14, 82; Greater Prague, 14, 83; under Habsburgs, 83, 92-3, 99; housing shortages, 56-7, 63; under Hussites, 87-8; motto, 179; patron saint, 5, 29, 120; pollution, 122, 170, 172, 178; population, 5, 14, 56, 83, 169, 170; scale model, 116; Town Hall and civic affairs, 167-72, 176-7; urban growth, 83, 103, 116, 120-1, 169; views and visual delights, 5, 56, 78, 84, 103, *104-5*, 106, 123; *see also* Praguers *and under individual place-names*
Prague Castle: 16, *18*, 26, 87, 90, 91, 101, 103-7; "Hunger Wall", 81
Prague National Committee (city council), 167-70, 176-80
"Prague Spring" Festival, 135-6, *136-7*, 155
Praguers: birthrate, 169-70; as car owners, 41, *173-5*, 179; civic responsibility shown by, 41, 184; as commuters, 39, 178-9; dress, 42; in exile, 28, 60; humorous sayings, 13, 18, 29, 44, 58; quality of life, 41-2, 44-6, 51-8, 60-1; as subject people, 6-7, 24, 28, 41, 58, 181; weekend exodus, 54, 55, 56-7, 61, 63, 74-5; *see also* Labour and employment
Přemyslid dynasty, 7, 78, 82, 106
Primátor (Lord Mayor) (interviewed), 167, 168, 169, 170, 172, 176-7
Protestants: 82, 83, 92, 125; versus Catholics, 77, 88, 90; Reformation, 88

R
Religion, state control, 111, 115, 119, 133; *see also under individual denominations*
Rudolf II, King, 83, 90, 91, 104, 106, 154

S
Sadová, Battle of, 93
Shops and shopping, 31, *36*, 42, 44, *44-5*, 45-6, 56
Sigismund, King, 82, 86, 87
Slánsky, Rudolf, 13
Slapy, 55, *62-75*
Slovakia: 5, 6, 10, 82, 97, 100; as Federal Republic, 6; writers, 16; *see also* Czechoslovakia
Smetana, Bedřich: 134, 135, *140-1*, 141-2, 144-5, 146, 147, 148; *Má Vlast* cycle, 136, 145
Smrkovský, Josef, 17, 26, 28
Sokol movement, 83, 93, 97, *100*
Soviet Army: 8, 13, 21, *21*, 24, *24-5*, 26, *26*, 28, 57-8, 181; occupation of Prague, *24-5*, 26, 28
Soviet Union: 21; alliance derided, 58; economic aims, 16; invasion, 28, 83
Sport: 53-4, 55, 152; ice-hockey, 54, *55*; soccer, 54, 55; Strahov sports complex, 157; swimming and boating, 54, *58*, *64-5*; *see also* Gymnastics, Sokol movement
Stalin, Josef: 13, 17, 18; memorial, *22*
Statues, *5*, *29*, *77*, *84-5*, *92*, *100*, 111, *127*
Strahov Monastery, 106, 108, *108-9*, 185
Street markets, 42, *44-5*, 177, *178*, 183
Streets and squares: Havelská, 42, *44-5*, 177, 183; Karlova, 115; Letenská, *108-9*; Malá Strana, 108; Na příkopě, 120, 181; Národní třída, 120, 135; Staroměstské náměstí (Old Town Square), 26, 48, 90, 99, 116, *118-19*, 133, 142; Václavské náměstí (Wenceslas Square), 5, 28-9, 46, 53, 120, 170
Student protests, 16, 23, 26, 28-9, 93
Suburbs: described by Kafka, 151; Karlín, 83, 120; Zabehlice, *122-3*, 174; Žižkov, 88, 188

Sudetenland, 10-11
"Švejk, The Good Soldier", 134, *144*, 150
Svoboda, Ludvík, President, 18, 23, 26, 28
Synagogues: *116*, 119; Old-New, 82, 119; Pinkas, 119-20

T
Tábor, 87, 99, 136
Theatres and concert halls: 152, 155, 167; Black, 152, 154; children's, 154; House of Artists, 176; National, 42, 83, 142, 144, 145; Smetana, 155; Tyl (Nostic), 53, 139, 141, 155
Thirty Years' War, 56, 83, 109, 119
Trade: 7, 14, 82; black market, 45, 183; lack of advertising, 181; trading corporations, 45-6, 181; *see also* Economy, Industry
Transport systems: 31, 42, 44, 167, 178, 179; air, 44; Metro, 180, 181; railways, *38-9*, 120, 179; taxis, 167, 178; trams, *30-1*, 108, 179
Turks, *see* Ottoman Empire

U
United States, Army, 13, 181
Universities: Charles (also Charles-Ferdinand), 7, 80-1, 82, 86, 92, 115, 172; German element in, 82; in Slovakia, 100; Technical, 172

V
Václav, *see* Wenceslas
Valdštejn, Albrecht Václav Z., *see* Waldstein
Vienna, 60, 88, 93
Vltava, River (Moldau): 5, *12-13*, 14, *58*, 63, 77; Barrandov pool, 54; bridges, *58*, 77, 84; Kampa Island, 123; Smetana's *Vltava,* 136, 145; Strelecky Island, *171; see also* Charles Bridge
Vyšehrad cemetery, *142*, 148
Vyšehrad, Fortress of, 6, 14, 82, 136

W
Waldstein, Albrecht, Count, 109, 111
Warsaw Pact: 18, 20, 24, 117; Bratislava communiqué, 26, 28
Wenceslas (Václav), "Good King" and Saint: 7, 78, 82; statue, 5, 29, 120
Wenceslas (Václav) I, King, 82
Wenceslas (Václav) IV, King, 82, 87, 92
White Mountain, Battle of the, 83, 90, 99, 104, 109, 134
Woodrow Wilson, 99
World War, First, 5, 83, 97-8
World War, Second, 8, 10, 11, 169; *see also* German occupation, Nazis and Nazism
Writers, playwrights and poets: 13, 16, 18, 92, 134, 152; Čapek, Karel, 101, 184; Havel, Václav, 83; Mňačko, Ladislav, 16; Palacký, František, 93; Seifert, Jaroslav, 21-2; *see also under individual names*
Writers' Union, 20, 60, 134

Y
Youth groups, 26, *66-7*, 176, *195*

Z
Zápotocký, Antonín, President, 13
Závodní Stráž (Factory Guard), 167, 168
Žižka, Jan, 82, 87, *88*
Zoo, 77

Colour reproductions by Gilchrist Bros., Ltd., Leeds and Scan Studios, Dublin.
Filmsetting by C. E. Dawkins (Typesetters) Ltd., London, SE1 1UN.
Printed and bound in Italy by Arnoldo Mondadori, Verona.